BREATHE LIFE INTO YOUR RIDING

BREATHE LIFE INTO YOUR RIDING

Transform Your Riding with Inspirational
and Innovative Breathing Techniques

JENNY ROLFE

J.A. ALLEN · LONDON

First published in Great Britain in 2012

ISBN 978 0 85131 984 1

J. A. Allen
Clerkenwell House
Clerkenwell Green
London EC1R 0HT

J. A. Allen is an imprint of Robert Hale Limited

www.allenbooks.co.uk

A catalogue record for this book is available from the British Library

Designed and typeset by Paul Saunders
Edited by Jane Lake
Front cover illustration by Annie Whiteley

Printed in China

Disclaimer
The author and publisher shall have neither liability nor responsibility to any person or entity with respect to any loss or damage caused directly or indirectly by the information contained in this book.

I dedicate this book to Barrie, Simon and Lisa,
with my love always; and to my very special stallions
and wonderful clients and students who have
so enriched my life

Contents

Acknowledgements

I gave my dear husband a huge thank you in my book, *Ride from the Heart*, never expecting that his infinite patience would be tested again, during the writing of yet another!

Thank you so much Barrie for reading, yet again, the entire contents of a further book.

You have also spent hours taking photographs, which now have quite a professional touch. We both love our life together and I promise here that we will spend more time in Portugal. Thank you for being my 'soul friend'.

My love and thanks to all my family, especially to both Simon and Lisa for their constant encouragement and love. Lisa has just become engaged to Paul – so welcome to our family Paul, with all our love. You both deserve the very best!

Lesley Gowers has offered me tremendous support and willingly given of her expertise. I have really enjoyed working with you, Lesley; another learning curve for me! Thank you so much for keeping me on track with my vision for this book.

I wrote to Jane Kidd, sending a selection of my articles which resulted in writing for the *British Dressage* magazine, over several years. I have felt extremely pleased and proud to write for *British Dressage* and would like to thank Jane for this opportunity. I very much appreciate Jane giving some of her precious time to read my book and prepare the Foreword for me. Thank you so much, Jane.

Also it has been a pleasure to work again with Jane Lake, who has an exceptional talent for finding just the right 'words' and she has helped me to express myself with more accuracy, yet also some artistry too. Thanks for your skill and creativity, Jane, which has helped so much in bringing this project together.

Annie Whiteley has provided the sketches at the beginning of each chapter and also some of the amazing paintings within the book. Annie you are so skilled and talented – it is almost possible to feel the horses you paint coming out of the canvas! It is always a pleasure to work with you.

Visit Annie's website www.annwhiteley.com for more information about her creative equestrian art and commissions.

Bob Atkins spent a day with us taking photographs and I believe he took a shine to our work and particularly to my stallion Delfin. This is reflected in the perceptive and artistic photographs which appear throughout my book. I am so grateful, Bob!

A special message here for my great friend and mentor, Ross Harper-Lewis. I would like to remember, with affection, her dear husband Tony, who so sadly passed away recently. Ross, I have rarely witnessed such loving commitment. You are a very special person!

Bridgette Anderson has been a lovely friend, full of wise advice. Thank you for your inspiration and support throughout the writing of this book.

My huge thanks to Sarah Edgecombe; it is so good to have you back here now. We really missed your initiative and thoughtfulness whilst you were away, but Jake now has a beautiful sister Freya.

You have a natural way with horses and have a great future ahead of you!

I wish to give a very special thank you to Ella-Jane Creasy and her mother Paula. It has so enhanced my book to be able to include Ella-Jane in some of the photographs. Ella-Jane is a very special young student who totally captivated the heart of my stallion, Delfin.

There have been so many wonderful friends and clients/pupils who have supported me through the writing of this book. It would be difficult to mention them all but it has been the inspiration and feedback from teaching that has guided me through this project. It has been their intuition, perception and open-mindedness which have brought to life my methods of training. They have all become an important part of my life.

Lastly, my love and thanks to my beautiful stallions who willingly teach people from far and wide, using their individual talents.

Delfin: my truly great spiritual professor, who has captivated the hearts of people around the world. You have such a generous depth of spirit, Delfin. You have become my horse of a lifetime.

Maestu: who constantly gives of his calm yet sensitive nature. He willingly shares his noble spirit and teaches a connection through breathing for the rider. Many have expressed admiration of his majestic energy and pride.

Habil: my latest star. He follows me wherever I go, showing such a connection with every breath or sigh. Thank you, Habil, for taking me further on my journey of exploration; for demonstrating collection, passage and Spanish walk from changes in breathing, all with your unique *joie de vivre*.

My grateful thanks go to the following photographers and artists for their wonderful contributions to the book, and to those who gave their permission for their photographs to be used: Bob Atkins; Mike Evans – www.michaelevansphotography.com; Linda Hayden; Bob Langrish – www.boblangrish.com; Ingela Larsson-Smith – www.lostchildrenoftheearth.com; Rafael Lemos; Jean Navarro; Lorna Richardson; Barb Riebold; Barrie Rolfe – www.spanishdressagehorses.com; Christine and Charles Taylor; Becky Turlington; and Annie Whiteley (sketches and paintings) – www.annwhiteley.com.

All photographs were taken by Barrie Rolfe with the exception of those listed below.

Bob Atkins: pp. 18, 22, 38, 40, 41, 46, 47, 51, 54, 60, 71, 110, 114, 124, 164, 167, 169 180; Mike Evans: p. 169 (artwork); Linda Hayden: p. 81; Bob Langrish: pp. 83, 105, 131, 133, 136, 141; Ingela Larsson-Smith: p. 65; Rafael Lemos: pp. 31 (both), 108, 109; Jean Navarro: p. 34; Barb Riebold: pp. 21, 24, 187; Lorna Richardson: p. 156; Claire Spelling: p. 100; Charles Taylor: pp. 42, 125, 154; Phil Mingo / Horse / IPC + Syndication: pp. 62, 75, 175

Annie Whitely – all chapter opening sketches plus the illustrations: pp. 29, 66, 158.

Foreword

Jenny Rolfe has been brave, putting into words and seeking to clarify concepts that are esoteric and that many in the down-to-earth equestrian world might ridicule. She is however expressing what a few have always felt and what increasing numbers are becoming aware of as a wonderful way of communicating with the horse. It is not an alternative but an addition to the training of a dressage horse and it can play a major or minor part in the work, according to the character and ambitions of the rider and trainer.

All can benefit from understanding more about the approach discussed in the following pages, and in these days when rollkur has done such damage to the image of dressage, at least partial adoption of the ideas is particularly valuable.

One of my favourite quotes was made by Albert Einstein who said: 'The intuitive mind is a sacred gift and the rational mind its faithful servant. We have created a society where we honour the servant and have forgotten the gift.' For me this book respects what the great man was talking about and we have much to gain from this.

Jenny brings a fresh dimension to training, identifying and using an invisible energy force that enables connection and control of the horse with harmony. That is the forgotten gift that Einstein is talking about.

She does it in a practical manner that is easy to understand. It is backed up by testimonies from a good variety of horses and riders who are able to illustrate her approach.

Many of us have been taught to breathe deeply when we are nervous, most obviously when we are about to go into the arena for a test. This helps to relax us and make us aware of our bodies that we need to use so subtly in the controlling of our horse. Jenny Rolfe goes much further than this using breathing as a directional force with amazing results.

Another feature of the book that impressed me was the emphasis on listening. In today's hectic world, goal setting has become very important and most seek to achieve them as fast as possible. Too often that key aspect of training is neglected: the fact that the horse can teach us and that we need to spend time listening to him before and even when we are imposing our will on him. For Jenny this is fundamental to her training.

Much of her early listening is done from the ground when the horse is loose. She demonstrates how all those aids we have come to depend on so heavily are not necessary in establishing connection and control.

For those who do not have the opportunities to become skilled or strong enough to train their dressage horses according to current fashions, and for many more who would like to enlarge and develop their current approach, this is a book that will open a door to another dynamic in dressage.

Jane Kidd

International dressage judge and rider, and author

Introduction

Several years ago if someone had told me that they could gain response from a horse by becoming aware of breathing and levels of energy, I may have been extremely sceptical. Without much thought, I was placing my human limitations on the mind and sensitivity of the horse.

I have discovered that when the rider enhances a natural pattern of deeper core breathing together with more grounded energy, it will instigate an immediate and profound response from the horse. If the rider is disciplined and consistent with this practice, it will not only enhance general health and well-being but open the doors for further exploration. This practice can become a life-changing and profound experience as the rider undertakes a journey of self-discovery. This experience will lead to deeper connection with the horse, on every level. The rider will feel empowered to explore the many possibilities that will be revealed. The study of natural posture awareness and breathing will become a journey towards lightness and harmonious balance. This will be the essence of the dance – as both spirits, of human and horse, will come together as one.

The power of breathing has a direct affect on how the human and equine body can function. Shallow, tense breathing results in tightness of muscles and limbs which restricts both mobility and coordination. The rider has so much to focus on, that if his body is restricted by shallow breathing, he cannot fulfil his aspirations of relaxed harmonious riding. I am very aware of this as I used to experience times when I was tight and unyielding when riding. I thought that I needed a more highly qualified trainer to help me, yet I now realise that first I needed more awareness of how I was sitting and breathing.

Once we begin to master our own state of mind, tension and balance, we will be in a place where we can more easily be taught, by both a trainer and the horse. We will be able to respond more effectively with fluidity within our body and greater focus of our mind.

It is possible to look aesthetically correct in a good position but the rider cannot be totally effective unless there is a true connection and energy exchange between himself and the horse.

If we can gain an understanding of core breathing, it will help us to achieve more poise, posture and core stability within our riding. There will be insufficient control over the important muscles of the abdominal area if we only breathe into the ribcage and chest muscles. If we inhale and exhale, using lateral breathing, thus using correct abdominal muscles, then a core of stability will be created. This will help us to locate our correct centre of gravity and balance.

In my first book, *Ride from the Heart*, I covered a logical progression of training from loose work through to more advanced classical riding. Since I wrote that book I have had the privilege of teaching students and clients from many different countries and shared mutual experiences of life and horses. Sometimes I would be asked a question, which made me dig deeper to give a simpler explanation of technique.

Students wanted to know why breathing awareness had such a profound impact on both humans and equines. Not only were they looking for answers but also a depth of understanding that would enable them to instigate a more harmonious connection with their own horses.

One of my clients had travelled to China to study Tai Chi and Chi Gong. He remarked that my clinics were very similar to a Tai Chi Master's class.

My experience had been gathered from my relationship with horses, who had become my teachers. I had not undertaken any formal training for these techniques. I felt, though, it would be beneficial to gather more information by reading the principles of Tai Chi and the subtle energy of breathing. I found that I had been on a journey akin to these philosophies – which really proves the truth within them – that connect us with nature.

The journey for me has raised my awareness and stimulated much emotion as I have watched people working with my stallions. Some students have left us with a greater sense of 'self' and connection, whilst for other people it has proved empowering and life enhancing. My horses have taken them to a deeper level in their life and helped them to find for themselves a meaningful path, which frequently meant a change of direction in their lives or the undertaking of a new challenge.

Fear is the opposite emotion to personal mastery and empowerment. If we lack confidence then we may be giving the horse signals of our fear. Often we are not aware of this. Personal development does not mean to gain false ego but a humble and open mind, prepared to expand, experiment and grow.

This book has been written to help the rider, not only to ride in good posture and balance but also to cultivate a deep sense of connection and feel. We look at subtle energy and how the senses of the horse are tuned in to a deeper level. Mankind, on the other hand, uses more verbal communication and is

not conscious of the many other dimensions that can create a connection.

The first part of the book looks at exercises to build awareness and core breathing from the ground. Once this discipline is understood, it can become a part of our demeanor on all levels. Riding becomes not only a physical activity but one which enhances us and our horses mentally, spiritually, emotionally and physically.

Throughout the chapters, I guide the reader towards the many possibilities of connection through loose work. This will lay the foundation of trust in the relationship both as a friend and a rider. When we learn to ride with trust, we can 'let go' and connect from our core with more lightness in our minds, hands and hearts. It is amazing how many of us without thinking will only offer the horse heavy hearts, hands and minds. Allowing hands often come from an allowing mind.

There is much responsibility here for the rider to become disciplined and develop personal awareness. My book encourages the rider to take full responsibility for this and reap the rewards of a more harmonious relationship with the horse.

We travel the path of training to develop the happy athlete. Training methods are explained which will advance the athletic ability of the horse whilst cultivating a feeling of confidence, trust and enjoyment for both the horse and rider.

Many people have said to me that they wished they had known these 'secrets' many years ago. Hence, my goals have been to pass on the deeper levels of communication that the horse has revealed to me.

I hope to communicate with some clarity my experiences and learning curve, as my quest is to enhance quality of life and connection for the good of the horse and the soul of the rider.

One of my clients, Rebecca Turlington, now living in the USA, wrote the study beginning overleaf, which gives an interesting account of her experiences, following a path of classical horsemanship.

opposite page
My stallion Delfin has become an inspirational teacher

My story with Maestoso Gabriola, 'Brio' – 29 April 2011

My story with Jenny came about quite unexpectedly while vacationing in Cornwall with my husband. We were staying at a bed and breakfast owned by a couple who raise horses and own a lovely Iberian stallion. During our stay at their home, our hostess showed me a copy of Jenny's book, *Ride from the Heart*. Upon returning home, I ordered the book from Jenny and found that I was captivated by the bond she had developed with her stallions through her unique method of communicating with them, combined with love, honesty, and mutual respect.

For over 20 years, my husband's job has necessitated us moving to various overseas postings throughout the world. In each new location, my passion for horses has led me to explore varying disciplines of riding and breeds of horses. Although such diversity has been interesting, I have found that my riding experience has lacked the consistency of qualified instruction and sound capable horses necessary for the development and progression of my riding skills beyond a 'recreational hobby'.

While living in Egypt, I was introduced to classical dressage through a friend from the United States. I immediately knew the direction I wanted my focus in riding to follow. For our remaining years in Egypt, I travelled to the United States for one and two week training sessions with a classical dressage instructor and Lipizzana breeder in Oregon. My instructor was mentored by one of the classical Masters from the Spanish Riding School in Vienna and adhered strictly to the training methods used at the SRS. Video tapes of these lessons provided me with tools to use on my Arabian gelding back in Egypt and further fuelled my desire to learn as much as I could about classical dressage. After one of my training sessions, I was offered the chance to purchase a colt from the first breeding of my instructor's prize Lipizzaner

→

Becky with Maestoso Gabriola, 'Brio'

stallion, which she had imported from Piber, Austria several years earlier and had trained through Grand Prix level. The colt's name was Maestoso Gabriola, or simply Brio – and so began my *true* discovery of classical dressage!

Brio remained in Oregon and, after his fourth birthday, was backed and commenced his initial training with my instructor there following the systematic methods of the Spanish Riding School. During this time, my husband and I moved from Egypt to England, and I found Jenny. After reading, *Ride from the Heart*, I knew that the deep communication, connection and trust Jenny had established with her stallions was what I wanted with Brio. That summer, I spent a weekend with Jenny and her beautiful stallions at her farm in Devon. Upon arriving, she immediately introduced me to the stallions: Delfin, Maestu, Beduino and a young new arrival, Ebano. She then proceeded to work with Delfin in his stall, demonstrating how to quietly obtain and *maintain* respect through body language, posture and breathing

→

techniques. We also worked on relaxation, core breathing and self-awareness to facilitate connecting with a horse. Next, Jenny brought Delfin out, and in the calm ambience of her arena, Jenny and Delfin began their dance. For me, watching the mirrored movements and 'play' as their conversation developed together and intensified, was truly magical.

Jenny then had me enter the arena to see if I could obtain a connection with Delfin. Only by completely surrendering *all* thoughts and focusing entirely on *feel*, could I allow myself to correctly experience the core breathing techniques – exhaling energy and inhaling power. When I was able to accomplish this, Delfin's look changed and we were able to connect. I was amazed at the intensity of this connection! Delfin allows you into his soul through his eyes …What an emotional moment for us both!

The following day, Jenny suggested I ride Delfin, as we had connected well from the ground and she believed that he could teach me more from the saddle. Jenny worked with me on position and breathing in walk, and then on transition to trot with core breathing alone. What an amazing teacher Delfin was! In sitting trot, he offered passage but he seemed more stilted through the right hind leg.

Jenny explained that Delfin was telling me that I was holding tension somewhere in my body and not 'allowing' him to move forward freely. By breathing in time to his trot steps, allowing my

Delfin allows you into his soul through his eyes
....

hips to move with his hind legs and remaining completely focused on sitting straight in the saddle, Delfin made the transition into a lovely swinging trot! He therefore revealed to me that I hold tension between my shoulder blades and in my left hip (the result of an old riding injury). Without Delfin to show me my weaknesses and Jenny to interpret them, I would still be riding with unevenness and stiffness – oblivious to the hidden tensions in my body! How very unfair to the horse!

Recently, we have left England and are now living in the southern United States. Although our journey has just begun, I have found Jenny's techniques essential to my developing relationship with Brio. He is a proud, confident and very clever fellow who loves interacting with people and with other horses, but his manners were lacking when he first arrived. Through core breathing and calm assertive body language, I have taught him to respect my space both in his stall and when in cross-ties.

The biggest challenge I have faced has been keeping Brio's attention focused during our work sessions together. All of his previous classical training took place in an indoor arena with solid walls, perfect footing and no visible distractions. Now, we work in an outdoor arena or a field where he can see and hear his pasture mates, who often come to the arena fence and watch our training sessions! Depending on the weather, footing is not always ideal and the sloping terrain of the pasture challenges Brio's balance with a rider. By incorporating Jenny's core breathing techniques into our daily training sessions, performing lots of transitions and lateral work, and by keeping our sessions short and fun, Brio stays focused much longer and our sessions are far more productive. Loose work and lungeing has been extremely helpful in preparing Brio both mentally and physically for our daily work. Although Brio's classical training always included lungeing prior to ridden work, the addition of core breathing to lungeing clarifies my aids, thus resulting in a more immediate response to half halt and upward or downward transition requests.

I have also found that Jenny's breathing techniques have been an immense help to me in heightening my self-awareness and restoring my self-confidence in challenging situations. By taking a slow deep breath into my core and then exhaling, I can now re-center my thoughts and open my mind to new solutions and situations before they become frustrating and escalate into a problem. Core breathing has enabled me to be prepared to take charge of a situation and instigate change in a calm and methodical fashion, whether I am out on a hack or working in the arena.

On a personal level, Jenny's teachings have 'empowered' me to believe in myself and to pursue my goals in life with confidence. I now have the ability to stop the busy thoughts in my head and to calmly re-center myself so I am prepared to really *listen* – to both my own thoughts and to those of my horse. With the tools Jenny has provided, Brio and I can begin to write our own story. After all, we have waited years to be together, and Brio has so much to tell me...

As Jenny says, 'The horse is our greatest teacher'.

Barb Riebold

Becky tunes in to listen and find harmony with Brio

My desire is for this book to touch the heart and soul, to open the mind of the reader. In this way the horse will live a life akin to his true nature, horse and rider will connect to become both teacher and pupil.

So, join with me and enjoy the journey. Have the courage to go not where the path may lead, but to **follow in the trail of his hoof prints.**

Horse and rider will connect to become both teacher and pupil

Chapter 1

Breathe the Connection – through Loose Work

Connect with a blending of spirits

— JENNY ROLFE

Loose work – the ultimate herd connection

Whenever we study a foreign language we need to look further than just learning verbal communication to gain true empathy. The whole new culture and environment is extremely important when we try to form a mutual connection. For instance if you learn Spanish, you should not only pick up the language but also find it helpful to become familiar with the culture, history and way of life.

When we are trying to communicate with the horse, time spent understanding equine habits, traits and character, will help us to empathise more fully, with his true nature and ways.

We have our natural traits of intelligence, curiosity, complexity of mind, ambition and will to learn. These qualities natural to the human species can be used to connect with our equine friends.

The horse has different gifts, such as a natural connection to the universe, his intrinsic desire to be part of a secure herd and his unencumbered equine spirit. Our natural paths are so different and yet if we take time to learn the language of the horse, we will come together in a powerful, life-changing way. The basis of our language has to change, as we try to think like a horse.

Have you heard the expression 'You cannot understand the mind of a man until you have walked in his shoes and trodden his path?' Well, try using this concept as you delve into the language of the horse and follow the trail of his hoof prints.

For us to understand why loose work is so important, we need to spend time observing the interaction of the herd. The loose work is a potent method of connection, which involves using our body language and power of intention to become the lead mare in the herd. Once we can mirror this behaviour of the herd, our relationship with our horse will be totally transformed. When the horse realizes that we can communicate in his language, he will gain security and respect and be willing to listen to our most subtle body language and breathing.

Following the trail of his hoof prints

I recommend that anyone who rides and trains horses, spends time watching ponies or horses in their herd, to tune into their language and interaction. This was my learning ground as a child when I spent endless hours roaming around with the herds of ponies in the New Forest. I felt at one with the herd and I was accepted by them. I was not consciously trying to learn, but I was just taking in and absorbing what was happening around me.

When we use our body language in the loose work we are trying to emulate the interaction in the herd. The lead mare, or matriarch, gives the discipline and she will command total respect from the herd. The stallion is the protector of his herd and looks after the important space around them. He will make them aware of predators and try to see off any young upstart stallions who might want to encroach on his mares.

In loose work we try to mirror the behaviour of the matriarch mare. If any youngsters are behaving badly she will turn her whole body towards them, directing her body language and

---

F**ollow the trail of his hoof prints**

The stallion is the protector of the herd

energy to drive them out of the security of the group. There the dejected youngster will stay, until she decides to allow him to venture back into the herd.

The submissive youngster will then try to move back into the herd, posturing meekly, with a lowered neck and gesturing with his mouth.

When we initially work the horse loose, we drive him away and maintain this intention until we can see that he is ready to connect with us. His inner ear will come back and he will start to lick and chew. He will lower his head and neck, demonstrating a more submissive stance. This natural approach to gaining submission is to be encouraged as it reflects the behaviour of the herd family. It is the path to training horses true to their nature and spirit. True submission will always come from the mind of the horse and not through any attempt from the rider, to fix a contact with his mouth.

Submission is from the mind

The key to communication

Over many years I have studied the profound benefits of time spent working and connecting with the horse from the ground. When we sit on the back of the horse we want him to feel tuned into our thoughts and connected to our minds. This becomes possible as a blending of spirits come together resulting from working loose from the ground.

Just for a moment consider your expectations when you first ride your horse. Do you wait for him to respond to your breath energy and thoughts of your mind or do you anticipate having to use strong aids of leg and hand before you gain any response?

Have you built a relationship where your horse is listening for changes in your energy and breathing and prepared to move from a breath?

When we understand more fully the natural language of the herd, we can be much more influential as both a rider and trainer.

Our human language involves some listening but more often we are expecting to be heard and we express our thoughts and opinions through verbal language. Frequently we give less credence to an awareness of body language.

The herd however responds immediately, in unison, to any slight changes in emotion, breathing and body position. Apparently studies have been made relating to the behaviour of a herd of elephants who have been proved to share signals of changes in their environment over quite a large distance. There would appear to be some telepathy in their language which is little understood by humans and I believe that horses have a similar language which responds very quickly to energy changes within their surroundings.

We are familiar with the power of radio waves, microwaves and mobile phones which all use invisible yet powerful currents of energy to allow connection. It has also been proved that the power of the spoken word can send a variety of positive or negative signals which can travel great distances.

All living creatures are linked by energy which radiates around us. We can create positive energy waves by the power of positive thought. In other words we have a power similar to the elephants

All living creatures are linked by energy that radiates around us

which is potentially untapped. Yet the horse is highly aware of the energy waves we create by our power of thought and word. This power can help to transform our communication as riders and trainers. If we understand how receptive the horse can be, at such a deep level, we can be more influential within the relationship.

Visualise, just for a moment, that you are looking over the gate of a field watching the antics of a spectacular young stallion who stands with blazing eyes and crested neck ready to challenge any rivals. He is telling the world that he is a king. Suddenly, there is a sound and he instantly responds with head and tail flying high. He moves in high suspension, his action portrays to the world his true magnificence of spirit and power.

This is the essence of the perceptive and vulnerable horse, the spirit of the creature we try to understand. We want to be true to his nature within our relationship and the methods we use to teach him. If we allow the horse to become our teacher and spend time listening to his spirit, he has important lessons for us which will enhance every aspect of our life.

The herd responds in unison

He portrays to the world his true magnificence of spirit and power

Lessons from the horse

Let us look at examples of how we can learn from the horse.

A client arrived to spend a day training with me and my stallions. Initially I took some time helping her to gain more self-awareness using several exercises on the ground. Then gradually I felt that she was ready to work with Delfin. Over years I have come to truly respect Delfin, my senior Spanish stallion, as a great equine professor who constantly gives of himself and is always ready to teach. During that time we have built the kind of relationship where I only have to walk into the school and he will mirror the energy of my breath. But this relationship has taken much time, patience and even more patience.

Alison started to work with Delfin, who was moving loose around her, and she was trying very hard to gain his full concentration. I encouraged her to begin with more assertive body language so that he would recognise her status as herd leader.

For several minutes Alison worked with Delfin, who trotted in a circle around her. I then asked her to calm her energy, lower her head and body stance and breathe more deeply inwards asking Delfin to come down to halt, but he would not respond. She couldn't understand why he refused to stop, as she had lowered her head, neck and shoulders and was offering him a place of relaxation. Delfin, however, being keenly observant, noticed that Alison still held a tight grip on the whip with a clenched fist and hand.

Most of Alison's body language was telling Delfin to relax but the tension in her arms and whip was still giving Delfin the signal to keep moving forwards.

As soon as she understood her mixed signals, Alison relaxed her hand and the whip was lowered, free of tension. Delfin then came down to halt and willingly faced Alison with a lowered head and neck to mirror her totally relaxed stance.

I instructed Alison to just take a deep outward sigh, but Delfin just continued to stand still watching her keenly. He did not respond and mirror her deeper sigh. I asked her if she had 'felt' the release of tension throughout her body when she sighed or

Delfin will mirror the energy of my breath

had she just taken a more superficial, mechanical sigh. She smiled knowingly, and then relaxed, as her tension had again increased. She could not believe that Delfin could possibly respond to such subtle changes in energy.

Alison then repeated a deep sigh, but now released her tension through a huge release of energy and within seconds Delfin became her mirror. He gave a deep exhalation and lowered his head and neck, standing in a very relaxed way. Both human and horse connected through a blending of spirits, opening the path to harmony and love.

I can also illustrate the power of the horse to connect with our inner emotions by mentioning someone called Liz, who was trying to work with Delfin at liberty. He chose to totally ignore her requests and continued to walk around the arena as far away from her as possible. Liz was deeply upset as he just totally switched off and ignored her presence in the school.

I had not experienced this situation before so I decided to put Delfin back into his stable and consider what we could do next.

I just stood in the school and chatted with Liz who was rather tense and I felt she was holding something back. We exchanged thoughts for quite a while about riding, horses and how we can communicate. I did not feel that I was connecting with her innermost feelings so I rather apprehensively mentioned to Liz that I sensed she was withdrawn and not allowing herself to 'let go'. Immediately the flood gates opened; she was crying and then apologising for her tears.

Liz was experiencing a traumatic situation in her personal life and she continued to express her anxiety, sadness and fear. Her husband had told her only a few days before the clinic that he intended to leave her and the family. Liz was totally shocked but some strong inner intuition and conviction drove her to still come and meet us, although she felt totally overwhelmed by the crisis.

I listened for a while, rather stunned and unsure what to do next. I then suggested that we bring Delfin back into the school, but Liz was very apprehensive about how he would respond. She did not want to experience rejection, yet again!

> Human and horse connect through a blending of spirits

The spirit of the horse

Only the spirit of the horse could now intervene.

This was to be a steep learning curve for me as I started to watch Delfin, who was now both responsive and willing to interact with Liz. He listened to her breathing and body language and calmly and obediently worked around her on the circle in walk, trot and canter. In this way Delfin was able to demonstrate that, initially, he could find no place for calmness or communication. When she was able to express her feelings and release through her tears, she opened herself up to connection and communication where both pleasure and peace could enter.

I watched as they both came together, dancing as one. I saw more tears from Liz, but this time it was an expression of sheer elation! She was so moved that Delfin gave so much and he was helping her to find joy and an inner peace amongst the turmoil of her situation. What a teacher! What a gift from God!

The horse is extremely perceptive and we may deceive humans with a cheerful expression but the horse will pick up on the reality of our feelings.

These become precious moments to treasure as we feel the presence of a kindred spirit. This is the way God meant for us to influence the horse. In this way both human and horse can grow in spirit and love.

Both human and horse connect through a blending of spirits

There is much of value to learn from the work on the ground as we learn to listen to the horse and become more aware of tension and how it affects us physically. These important lessons can be so helpful as once in the saddle our enhanced awareness will encourage a true and natural empathy with the horse.

WHAT THE HORSE HAS TAUGHT US SO FAR

Let us now take a look at what we have learnt so far.

1. The horse will be very sensitive to our thought-energy waves.

2. He will immediately be aware of our emotions including those of confidence or fear.

3. He will tune into our body language and detect any tension held in our body.

4. He will be totally receptive to our breathing whether it is shallow and tense or more rhythmic core breathing.

5. He will read accurately our power of intention.

6. The horse is looking for a leader who is calm, self-aware and confident.

The foundation for the future

I have studied the nature of horses all of my life and I am totally convinced that the more harmonious relationships are not only built from work under saddle but also from valuable time spent observing the horse at liberty. I have learnt the significance of building a bond of trust and leadership from the work on the ground.

This is also a good opportunity to teach the horse to become both focused and athletic when working at liberty. During these methods of training he can quickly learn to accept our leadership and our ability to make decisions. This will help him to gain the security and direction he would naturally seek within a herd.

Each rider who comes to me for training with their horse will begin by working the horse from the ground. All the tack will be removed and the horse will be turned loose in the school, whatever their previous level of training.

It is so important to see the horse in his natural state with no tack and observe his responses and reactions. This will make all training under saddle much more harmonious and effective. The loose work alleviates much potential for confrontation, which could be demonstrated under saddle. The horse who appears uncooperative or resistant under saddle will quickly become willing and relaxed when we communicate in his language through the loose work.

I spent some time in Southern Ireland working with a Spanish stallion who had viciously attacked several people including his rider and his groom. I felt some trepidation at first but I knew I had to be focused and effective from the first moment I met this horse. I made the decision to work with him at liberty to discover his true nature and for him to learn to trust and respect me. He was insecure, dominant and attack had become his first line of defence. After a week of loose work and riding he calmed and connected and became a much more content horse. He is still with his owner who has continued this loose work within his training. His full story is contained in my book *Ride from the Heart*, as he taught me many lessons which would change my path of training and teaching for the future.

Loose work alleviates much of the potential for confrontation

Lessons from Beduino

Let us look at the value of loose work with my young Lusitano colt, a stunning palomino, Beduino. He has been with us since he was two years old and I have found through every stage of his development that working loose has brought huge benefits. As a young colt he could be energetic and challenging at times. He showed no malice but exerted only natural curiosity and pride. The pattern of behaviour in the herd is for colts to engage together physically to ascertain the hierarchy for the future: which colt will be a future leader? This quest will be pursued throughout their lives as each colt looks to become a leader for their own herd of mares and offspring.

The most successful method I have found, between human and horse, is building a bond of mutual connection and trust through the loose work.

I am neither tall nor physically strong and certainly do not seek major confrontation with any horse. I would rather establish my leadership and identity within his herd, through this mutual connection based on respect and trust. This relationship is invaluable to me when training a young stallion or a horse of any sex or breed. The connection and respect has to be built 'mind to mind'.

Let us look at a sequence of events which occurred on one particular day when I was loose schooling Beduino. He had not been worked for a few days and he entered the school with rather too much exuberant, high energy. I let him off the rope and he galloped away to enjoy his freedom paying little attention to me. I then encouraged him to move forward using my body language to support his play.

Becoming rather cheeky, he then cantered across the school to talk to my lovely bay stallion Maestu, as his stable adjoins the indoor-school area. There are some metal bars that separate the stallions but they can still see each other and talk to each other. It is part of their education that they learn to concentrate in the school, rather than being allowed to talk to their friends. My older stallions understand the boundaries and do not attempt to communicate when they are working in the school.

> Build a bond of mutual connection and trust through loose work

My stallions can always greet each other unless they are working in the school

Communicate with a focus on body language and power of intention

I therefore quickly applied a total focus of my body language and power of intention to drive him away from Maestu's stable but, on this particular day, I was far too slow with my responses and Beduino was enjoying an extremely noisy conversation with Maestu.

I quickly became more assertive and directed all my focus towards Beduino. I began to drive him around in a circle and then I blocked his path to change direction before he arrived back in close proximity to Maestu.

Gradually he began listening to me as I directed his thoughts and energy. I then tried another tactic; I directed Beduino to circle around me, allowing him to trot extremely close to Maestu's stable. As he approached this area, which had provided much distraction, I directed more pressure with my body language, breathing and supported this with a crack of the whip. He was now tuned in to my power of intention. His thoughts were directed away from Maestu and he was listening most intently to me.

The noise of the whip was to attract his attention and made no contact with him. I sometimes use a shampoo container with a few small stones rattling inside. This noise will attract attention. I do not work in a small pen but use a large arena and so I sometimes need extra help at the beginning of a session to gain a focus towards me.

I watched Beduino intently with every stride to see if his concentration waned. If he turned his head outwards or ignored me, just for a second, I would again direct more pressure towards him.

I only accepted the situation when his full attention was on me alone and I did not allow other noises or horses to disturb his concentration. I also used the power of my total focus on him. I observed his energy closely and if I saw his movement slow down or his attention waver, I responded instantly and re-enforced my driving energy.

Beduino was learning in this way that I was the lead mare, the matriarch of the herd, who commanded his total attention and respect and yet also his trust. He was learning to respect my authority, in a natural way, as a more assertive member of his family.

After a few minutes I sensed a change in Beduino as he circled around me. He became totally tuned in to my breathing alone. An outward breath increased his energy and an inward breath brought him down into walk. I no longer needed much body language and certainly no noise from my whip. He was responding to my breathing and slight changes in my body stance. Less was becoming more.

I then encouraged him to walk close to Maestu. I was about fifteen metres away from Beduino as he walked very close to Maestu's stable. He showed no lapse in connection to me or even changed the energy or rhythm of his walk. He was now totally connected to me. As he walked past Maestu again, I took a deeper inhalation to ask him to halt and relaxed my shoulders and head. Beduino turned into the circle to face me, just a couple of metres from Maestu who was standing behind him watching us closely.

He showed no further interest in Maestu but was totally responsive to my body position and any subtle changes in breathing.

In this way I formed a connection, mind to mind, an invisible bond of leadership, respect and trust. If this bond can become

As the horse responds to your breathing, less will become more

Create an invisible bond of leadership, respect and trust
....

established before you sit on the back of the horse, the ridden work becomes only an extension of this friendship.

The lessons from Beduino are simple yet fundamental.

1. The importance of becoming a focused true leader – commanding total attention.

2. Understanding how to feel bold and disciplined, with clarity of mind.

3. Learning to react and respond quickly. There is no time for indecision.

4. The importance of a complete focus with the intention of connecting with the mind, spirit and energy of the horse.

5. As the relationship grows, developing the ability to predict potential actions and respond accordingly.

6. Being patient and yet positive, worthy of both trust and respect.

You will need to be very assertive at first to gain total attention and respect. Once the horse understands your qualities of leadership together with your reassuring calm body language for connection, he will be ready to listen to just whispers of breathing. You will give part of your inner self and become linked, mind to mind and soul to soul, with the horse. You will learn the important lessons of the herd which are also profound lessons for **life**.

The lessons of the herd are profound lessons for life

Training the horse to become an athlete

I have found loose work to be an invaluable tool of training whether you are teaching a young horse or working with a horse more advanced in his years and level of training.

Time spent watching the horse at liberty will give valuable direction when planning the future of his training. This is an opportunity to assess his natural movement and his general athletic ability. Also we can assess the responses and reactions as well as his energy level and state of mind.

We will learn to understand the natural mechanics of movement when we work with the horse with no tack or restriction and just watch him demonstrating his true nature and ability. Over time we will begin to tune into the spirit, emotions and individual nature of the horse to become more effective as trainers.

Loose work is an opportunity to assess the movement and natural ability of the horse

Engagement, submission and collection are all part of the natural movement of the horse. When he learns to respond in this way with only mind-to-mind connection, the aids of the rider will become less rather than more.

The horse seeks natural balance and when ridden this will be enhanced by a good natural balance of the rider. If the rider constantly alters his balance with strong leg or hand aids, this will be extremely unsettling for the horse trying to move in a regular rhythm.

Subtle communications will be learnt, taught and exchanged during the time spent working from the ground.

Sometimes work under saddle can manifest problems, for instance resistance in movement, lack of impulsion or problems with contact. These problems can be addressed under saddle but, importantly, watching the horse at liberty will add a new dimension within training. You will see how the horse responds and adapts your aids and energy accordingly. For instance, the horse may feel too restricted when ridden, with too much pressure from the reins. His delicate mouth may feel tight with forced contact which creates a lack of confidence when the horse moves forward into a restricting hand.

A relaxed neck and head is the result of a relaxed mind using sufficient energy in physical movement.

Energy can be born of fear and flight or it can be an expression of pleasure and pride for the horse. The horse was born to move and when he is confined to a stable and only allowed movement under a rider, this is most unnatural for him. His character yearns for physical freedom and yet a desire for connection with his herd.

> A relaxed head and neck is a result of a relaxed mind

A **relaxed** head and neck is a result of a relaxed mind

Over several months I spent some time teaching loose work to a young, unbacked, Fell stallion. We then commenced work on the lunge and when we decided the time was right, we began some light ridden work, on the lunge.

When his rider initially sat on his back, he remained quite relaxed and immediately walked and trotted from her breathing alone. He had already connected in this way from the relationship on the ground. His first experience as a ridden horse was to tune in to her breathing. This was a profound experience for both the rider and myself.

I also worked with a big Spanish yearling colt who had travelled to our yard from France. We took him into the school to explore his new home and it took less than five minutes for him to circle around me with a total connection to my breathing. I never fail to feel a deep thrill of excitement when each new horse connects in this powerful way.

Good communication between horse and rider is fundamental for the future of any successful programme of training. The horse lives within the moment, and to gain a positive response it is helpful for us to put aside problems from the past and concerns for the future when we are working with him. When we connect with the horse at liberty, all our thoughts and focus are with the horse, in that moment of time. This discipline is an excellent way for us to learn the power of intention, together with a focus on core breathing.

Let us look at loose work now, not only as a valuable tool for connection, but also as an important foundation within a training programme, based on building harmony and trust.

> This discipline is an excellent way to learn the power of intention with a focus on core breathing

Advantages of loose work for the trainer

1. A time to learn more of the natural herd language.

2. The development of self-awareness of personal body language and breathing to enhance every communication with the horse.

3. An opportunity to acquire skills of leadership and demonstrate the power of intention.

4. A time to observe the horse – his mood and way of moving.

5. Learning to work with the personality of the horse – gaining more understanding of his individual 'horse language'.

6. An opportunity to gain the attention of the horse – this pattern of learning and communication will then be reflected in work under saddle – hence confrontation is minimised.

7. Connecting with the horse through core breathing – to be enhanced by riding.

Advantages of loose work for the horse

1. An effective and natural method of warming up.

2. An opportunity to let off steam with no tack – his natural exuberance can be unleashed without restriction; he is allowed to be a horse.

3. A chance to communicate with the rider in a very natural way for him.

4. To acknowledge the trainer/rider as the herd leader.

5. An opportunity to connect with the trainer whilst enjoying freedom in movement.

6. Learning how to move in good natural balance.

7. It helps to build the correct muscles to support the extra weight when carrying a rider.

8. Learning to work with steady core breathing – the key to balance and harmony for both horse and rider.

9. Understanding how to release excess tension with a deep sigh. This will enable further work to continue through a spine that is mobilised and a ribcage that is not contracted.

Loose work is an opportunity to assess the ability, energy and individual nature of the horse and also the way in which he naturally uses himself. He may be naturally rather lazy or demonstrate a very high level of energy. We may observe him lacking energy in his gaits with insufficient propulsion from the hind limbs. Insufficient activity will cause the head and neck carriage to become elevated, but as we ask for more energy within the gait, the horse will produce greater self-carriage and fluidity within his movement. This will result in a natural (not artificial) lowering of the head and neck carriage. This 'frame' can be the basis of warming up the horse under saddle. If the horse can learn to move with fluidity and relaxation in loose work this way of going can be continued under saddle. Once you have observed the way of working during the time spent at liberty, it will give you more direction once you are in the saddle.

> Loose work is an opportunity for the horse to learn to work with steady core breathing

The horse is lacking energy causing his head and neck to be elevated

Body awareness in loose schooling

If we want to work with a calm horse, we need to be 'body aware' from the moment we enter the stable or arena. When we walk steadily and calmly, breathing in a relaxed way, the horse will sense our mood and respond with a more confident attitude. When we relax and steady the mind, the body will follow and the horse will not feel intimidated. The voice can be gentle to calm the horse.

There will be occasions when more assertive body language and a dominant tone of voice may be used to establish leadership. We need to be consistent in our actions because this is the way the horse will learn. We will mirror the behaviour of the herd that would naturally offer the horse companionship and security.

The body language used in loose work mirrors the herding instinct of the horse. The leader of the herd controls space and energy. If for instance a dominant mare feels a youngster is disrespectful she will chase him at speed out of her personal space and maybe out of the security of the herd. In the wild, the youngster in this exposed situation outside the herd would be at greater threat from attack. A predator will always attack a horse in its most vulnerable area just behind the withers because the horse cannot easily reach this area to bite or kick in self-defence. It is, therefore, incredible that horses allow humans (potential predators) to sit in this vulnerable spot.

I direct my body language, breathing and focus to this area behind the shoulder, down towards the ribcage of the horse. This is the place where the legs of the rider will hang. Breath and body

We will mirror the behaviour of the herd

I direct my body language, breathing and focus towards this area behind the shoulder

energy are used in loose work and, when under saddle, replaced with the relaxed breathing legs of the rider. When the horse feels the energy of our body language and breathing, directed in this manner, he will naturally move away from the impetus.

Loose-schooling technique

To practice the following techniques you will need a well-fenced arena, an indoor school or a round pen.

Imagine a 20m x 40m arena divided into two. Ideally two handlers will stand on the centre line of the arena, each about 10m (33ft) from the short side of the school.

Each handler will be responsible for encouraging the horse forward at their end of the arena. On the left rein, you will hold the whip in the right hand and adopt a position as if lungeing. Position your body so that your right shoulder and arm is herding the horse, following up behind him. Your body is positioned facing the flanks of the horse. You will be using your body language, breathing and core energy directed to the area just behind where your leg would hang if you were in the saddle.

> The breath and body energy in loose work is replaced under saddle by the breathing legs of the rider

Position your body so that your right shoulder and arm is herding the horse

The energy is an invisible but potent connection from your core directed towards the horse. The outward breath is similar to the feel of a ball bouncing up and out of your core and directed towards the horse.

On the left rein you will step towards the horse using the outward breath to encourage him to move forward. Your left hand will guide him around the circle as if drawing in an imaginary rope. Your right shoulder and arm will follow the horse around and the whip, which is held in your right hand, will hang lightly and low, to be used only if more impulsion is needed.

Just visualise a triangle. The horse represents the base line. You are standing at the top point of the triangle embracing the whole of the horse. Your left side guides the base of the triangle. Your core breathing directs energy towards the base whilst your right shoulder, arm and whip follow up behind the base. The horse instinctively moves away from assertive, herding, body language. Your power of intention and focus will be felt by the horse so remember to emulate the behaviour of the herd matriarch and be determined that the horse will move energetically away from you.

Direct the horse around one half of the arena towards the other handler who uses his body and whip position to keep herding the horse forward, around his short side of the school and on down the long side again.

If the horse is lazy then encourage more energy and *joie de vivre*. The over-exuberant horse should be loose schooled until he finds a steady rhythm and begins to relax.

The horse will soon adapt from using the whole school to circling around one of the handlers as if on the lunge. The first handler can take over around the short side of the school and encourage the horse onto the circle around him. The horse will soon learn to respond to the handler's position, which directs him to work on a circle as if he were being lunged, but with no lungeing equipment.

The second handler uses the whip, holding it out towards the long side facing the path of the horse, in order to block his path down the long side and encourage him to maintain the circle. The

Your power of intention is felt by the horse

horse is encouraged to continue working on a circle with a feel of connection as the breathing and body language of the handler control the energy of the movement.

When the horse begins his work there is often little connection but as he feels your energy giving direction, he will start to tune in to your breathing patterns. As soon as you see his inside ear flicking backwards and his neck begin to lower, you know

The first handler encourages the horse to work on the circle whilst the second handler blocks the path of the horse
....

Continue working on the circle until the horse seeks a connection
....

that he is seeking the connection with you. He will become more attentive and soon will respond to your breathing alone.

If you notice the horse is still tight in the jaw then relax your own jaw and gently chew. I have found that most horses quickly mirror this relaxation and begin to release the jaw and soften through the mouth.

Your outward breath will transmit energy which will instigate more energy or an upward transition. The deeper inward breath will slow and steady the horse, into a downward transition. If the horse does not respond to these breathing techniques together with the body language, the voice and whip can be used to re-enforce the command.

The response time varies with each horse: a more dominant horse may take longer to respond, as will a more energetic horse. When you notice the horse is seeking the connection with the lower neck, relaxed jaw and inside ear flicking backwards, just slow your walk and take a deep breath inwards. Relax your fingers and lower your whip and turn your body away from the horse, facing slightly inwards towards the centre of your circle. You will then find that the horse will stop and turn in to face you.

When I ask the horse to halt, I lower my head and shoulders as I ask the horse to join me in a place of calmness. When he comes into halt, I then take a deep outward sigh. The sigh is a total release, down through the body, a grounding and letting go of tense energy. The horse will recognise this release and he will know whether you have really 'let go' – in which case he will mirror this, releasing his own tension with a sigh or blowing through his nostrils – or whether you have only created a superficial mechanical action.

I must add that many horses are extremely perceptive and tune in extremely quickly to the techniques of breathing.

When you approach the horse, walk with a lowered head and relaxed shoulders, keeping your whip softly lowered in your hand. The posture should be relaxed and inviting. The horse should be encouraged to stay on the circle and not to walk into the centre to the handler, unless invited. If the horse begins to walk in, you can use assertive body language by moving towards him to encourage

> Your outward breath will transmit energy. The deeper inward breath will draw in energy to steady the horse

> Take a deep outward sigh – the horse will mirror your release

him to maintain his position on the circle. Throughout the loose schooling, the horse will be constantly giving us signals which will help us to understand his responses and nature more fully.

When the horse is moving away at our request with his inside ear flicking backwards and forwards with an expression of concentration we know we are connected with his mind. If he raises his head because something distracts him, we need to quickly reinforce our authority with our body language, voice and breathing.

The power of this connection is enormous and can benefit hugely the relationship and harmony sought by all dressage riders and trainers in all disciplines.

On the following pages are some of my case studies where the value of loose work has effectively transformed both the relationship and performance of both horse and rider.

I lower my head and shoulders and ask the horse to join me in a place of calmness

CLARE AND LAURIE, WARMBLOOD GELDING

One of my clients, a keen competitive rider, came to me with her five-year-old, 17hh, Warmblood gelding. He appeared to lack any motivation or confidence in forward movement. I felt he had been rather restricted within his neck by the rider's hands and he was also a large-striding horse. This was giving the rider the feel of a 'hovering' movement but he was not using himself with sufficient energy.

Over several days we worked him loose in the school, encouraging him to move with more energy and impulsion. He began to release and flow through his spine, and his forward movement gained in confidence and fluidity. His neck began to stretch and lower from the withers and he lengthened the muscles through his top line.

When he became confident and more athletic in his loose work we began lungeing using loose side reins, some-times using trotting poles to continue to encourage the release through the spine and the downward stretch through his neck.

We then brought the rider and horse together on the lunge, with the rider more focused on her top-to-toe awareness (see Chapter 3) and core breathing to maintain her stability and balance.

Initially, Clare rode with longer reins with a focus on her seat and core connection only. Then she rode transitions, again initiated through her core breathing. Her horse began to offer more lightness through a relaxed back, active limbs and a more arched and lengthened neck which came up and out from the withers into a truly released poll. He was learning to become an athlete and responsive, confident pupil.

Gradually they built confidence together with more harmonious aids, both listening and tuned in to more sensitive communication.

A focus on top-to-toe awareness and core breathing will enhance stability and balance

Author's Case Study 2

CAROL AND HER BAY STALLION

My client, Carol, arrived with her stunning bay stallion in a beautiful horsebox. He was led off the horsebox having travelled for several hours, already tacked up in a bridle and a *serreta*, an unyielding metal noseband. Carol carried a whip in her left hand as she off-loaded her stallion, and I could quickly see the dominant role of this lovely horse and the nervousness of his owner. I asked if he could be taken straight into my school and have all his tack removed. She looked anxious and rather reluctantly left me in the school with her stallion.

I used all my energy directed towards him as he had to learn first to move away from me. He galloped and bucked with huge energy for several minutes around me. I decided the time was right to make him more aware of me again so I blocked his path a couple of times to change his direction.

Within minutes he was circling around me listening to my breathing energy and responding to both my inward breath and outward breath. When we came to halt I stood giving a deep sigh which he mirrored. Then he began to follow me around the school.

The following day when we took him back into the school, I asked Carol to lunge him. She said he often bucked on the lunge but on this day, he proceeded to work calmly on the lunge with good concentration and energy. He was content to focus on Carol. She then began to work him under saddle. He continued giving her calm and steady energy, only wanting to please his rider.

I had spent several hours working with Carol on the ground helping her to gain more self-awareness top to toe. She was well prepared to connect with her stallion with a focus on core breathing once in the saddle. Both Carol and her stallion were able to settle down and learn as both were focused and responsive to each other.

The session went well as they learnt to listen and synchronise with each other, both having acquired much from the time spent on the ground. Carol had gained self-awareness and more confidence whilst her stallion gained security through his loose work. They were now well equipped to start on a new journey of empowerment and discovery.

Author's Case Study 3

LOUISE AND HER BLACK STALLION

Louise came to stay with us for several days bringing with her a lovely young black stallion. She enjoyed hacking out with him but in the school he would not go forward and if she became strong with her aids, he would rear, buck and spin around, totally opposed to moving forward. This happened daily until Louise lost confidence in taking him in her school. Until she arrived with him I was unsure what might be the cause.

I always work horses loose before I teach ridden work in order to assess the personality and movement of the horse without the rider. This work reduces potential conflict as very often resistances within training are not always solved easily by the mounted rider.

This black stallion was a stunning and strong-minded horse who did not wish to connect in the loose work easily. I used my body language to get him to move forward but he appeared inattentive for many minutes. I then had to block his path several times before he took me seriously as someone who could be an important part of his herd. He was athletic and forward-moving in my indoor school and, whilst he was working at liberty, did not put up any of the resistances Louise had mentioned.

Loose work can reduce potential conflict under saddle

→

Author's Case Study 3

I then spent considerable time with Louise and found that she was quite strong in her arms and wrists and had not been aware of the tightness she offered when riding. Out hacking she was more relaxed but her own tension rose in the school with the pressure of trying to achieve the right outline and way of going.

I decided to lunge Louise so that she could tune in to riding from her core only with the lightest of connection with the reins.

The following day we worked her stallion again at liberty, until he relaxed and offered to connect with me, before lungeing him with Louise in the saddle. She had gained much more awareness on the previous day, learning exercises from the ground. I wanted her now to spend a few minutes, once in the saddle, going through her basic posture awareness, top to toe.

I then took off the lunge line and put on some classical music to create a relaxing atmosphere in which Louise could continue her riding. I recommended that she ride for a few minutes with the reins in one hand only. In this way her body and core could maintain stability and energy flow with less focus and tension in her arms and hands.

Louise was riding forward and covering the ground with more enthusiasm now. Once she had seen that her stallion did not spin around in the school whilst working loose or on the lunge, Louise gained more confidence to allow him to move forward. Slowly her self-assurance grew as he showed no resistance or thought of rearing or bucking.

Interestingly, I had two spectators who had come especially to watch how we tackled a horse with problems in the arena. They did find it hard to believe the progress after only two sessions of loose work plus a rider session of relaxation and core breathing. They were hoping to see more high jinks in the school and how we coped with them!

Louise returned home to her own school and continued making steady progress with her training. She has written to me often to say that her path of horsemanship was totally transformed and her journey towards harmony truly began over those days.

Chapter 2

The Path to Personal Empowerment

> Our path is shaped by faith, hope and a love that moves mountains
>
> — JENNY ROLFE

My journey

A few years ago a friend gave me a saying, which read:

> 'Do not go where the path may lead, go instead where there is no path and leave a trail.'
>
> — RALPH WALDO EMERSON (1803–82)

My friend understood the challenges I was facing each day, exploring and delving into innovative ways to feel a closer bond with my horses. Many days I have ventured into the unknown looking for a deeper connection, seeking unity with the true spirit of the horse.

Some days proved inspirational but in the early days I had little self-confidence though an inner force was guiding me to try and unravel some of the mystery of communication. I gave no more than a listening ear to the messages given to me by my stallion. Some days I found it hard to believe that with love in my heart and awareness of my breathing, a horse would tune in with such a deep connection. Was this my imagination or would this bond lead to more profound revelations, as time passed by?

I was leaving the conventional path of my training technique and launching on an expansive voyage of discovery. I believe personal empowerment gives a sense of freedom of spirit and adventure. If we do not feel empowered from within, we often are fearful of the reaction of others to what we may do or say. It can stifle our unique talent when we give too much credence to the reaction of others. A spirit of self-belief and empowerment gives you the courage to be 'uniquely you' and God made us all as individuals.

Self-empowerment means to me, self-mastery, which is not borne of arrogance but in the spirit of humility. When you attempt to connect with the universe, it can only make you feel humble as you realise you are a very small part of the whole of creation. Yet, are we not linked together by spirit, love and experience so that we can share experiences. In this way we become part of the whole, not because we have superior knowledge but because we are willing to share, for the good of humanity. This is what can give us the feeling of personal empowerment.

Over the years we have kept Jacob sheep on our farm which cling together as a herd, but equally if one or two sheep wander off, the rest of the herd follow. It seems to be their nature to follow without question. Children at school yearn to be accepted and often socialise in groups. They may quickly lose confidence if other children pick on them for anything that appears different or unique: physical size or hair colour, for instance, or even great academic potential. A rift can be caused between children who view anything out of their 'box' as a threat to their self-esteem.

So to seek empowerment really means to develop and trust our unique identity, emotions, intuition and wisdom to be our own person, responsible for our own actions. It may mean branching out when no one else believes in you, yet your inner voice is saying something different. When you take the first step

> Self-mastery is borne in the spirit of humility

'out of the box' it can feel daunting and yet exciting and the universe can open up gifts for us all when we are true to ourselves and our spirit.

How can we be with horses and teach them to work, true to their individual personality, if we don't have the courage to be unique ourselves.

Delfin: a spiritual teacher

Delfin, my beautiful expressive Spanish stallion is well known as a true equine professor. He is a spiritual teacher who is always generous with his patience when working with people who come here for training. It was no surprise to find out that the ancestors of this incredible stallion were the original Carthusian horses who shared their lives with the monks from the Carthusian monasteries in Andalusia. This legacy is encapsulated within an intuitive equine spirit, capable of reflecting the truth of the soul of each individual he meets.

He evokes honest, raw emotion which can be so profound that it defies the language of words. He inspires a further dimension that creates the power of connection between the spirit of man and horse.

Delfin has helped me to define and acknowledge my fear. I had to be truthful with him and in return he taught me and helped me to find a path of empowerment. You cannot hide from fear but acknowledge it and say, 'well it's OK to feel nervous'. The strange part is that once recognised much of the worry and fear dissolves. We can then find a way to change the situation which is destroying our self-confidence. In this way we take responsibility for our own actions which can be a defining moment.

The horse just wants us to be ourselves and happy in our own skin! This lesson might seem very basic but it is also fundamental for life's journey, with or without our horses. This adventure, however, requires total honesty and regular discipline.

Over many years the relationship and understanding which has evolved with my stallion Delfin has totally transformed my previous philosophies. This equine professor has not only taught

> The equine spirit will reflect the truth of the soul

me a way to connect with every horse but he has been so gener-ous in teaching clients who travel to me from around the world.

During the early days I humbly taught trainers who had aspired to greater academic qualifications from more conven-tional training systems. When a rider has been taught for years to use strong rein and leg aids, there can be some scepticism when I talk about breathing as a connection.

Without a sense of purpose and belief, the lessons from my stallion could have dissolved as the sky might just fade insig-nificantly into the background of a painting. It was the response, always from the horse, which led me purposefully forward. Whenever I doubted my experiences the horse would show me how much he listened and reacted to my state of mind, thoughts, emotions and breathing.

Delfin — my great professor

Seeking a connection

Some clients arrive searching for a greater connection with their horses, together with lightness of aids in their riding. Others come as their horses have shown signs of aggression, anxiety and often a blend of mixed emotions. Many horses are mentally in a place where the human has found little connection and empathy. This can lead to mistrust and fear for horse and rider.

I always begin the training of every horse by working from the ground to say 'hello' and greet the horse in a like-minded language. The language of the horse is highly sensitive and he quickly tunes into a connection through core breathing. The only thoughts in my mind are to bond with the horse. There is no place for my ego or inflated self-esteem but neither will the horse find confidence with a person who is indecisive or lacking in self-worth. He is seeking someone who has self-belief. This does not mean that you know you are always right but rather that you listen to your inner wisdom and experience to make your decisions. You become a person who is comfortable in their own skin, accepting of human frailty yet conscious of deep inner strength.

You are a person willing to love, share and connect with the universe. This can facilitate a place where the horse can feel secure and comfortable. A place of harmony and peace, found deep within your heart and your soul.

The horse is willing to help you to gain personal empowerment. This does not mean the will to dominate but the capacity to build personal self-belief, joy, confidence and the courage to embark on a journey of exploration, together with your horse.

I now feel at home with each horse who is brought to me for training. I search to discover his personality through the loose work on the ground. I will then spend hours with the rider helping them to find a place of self-discovery and awareness. Empowerment can then begin, as both the horse and rider can come together, finding a point of connection mentally, physically and spiritually. This is a place where mutual empowerment can be nurtured and horse and rider can explore to reach

Listen to your inner wisdom

Connect
with the
universe
·················

out and grow. Both can gain confidence side by side as a deeper
bond of friendship and trust is built.

The challenge of training and riding the horse carries with it
a great responsibility to care for his welfare and comfort. If we
can learn to understand the nature and ways of the horse, we
can become more successful in achieving harmonious methods of
training. This will become the constructive path for teaching the
horse to gain his respect for our leadership whilst enhancing both
his trust and confidence.

The most fundamental principle of training is for us to nurture 'trust' which takes many months and years to build, but can
be destroyed in moments, by impatience and a lack of respect for
the horse. He may willingly be giving of his best but, with a vision
for success, we may be tempted to keep asking for more, which
can cause negative stress for both horse and rider. Whatever the
level of training it is very important to maintain a sense of fun and
joy within the discipline. Excess tension can become extremely
destructive, not only for performance but more importantly for

The most fundamental
principle of training is
to nurture trust

the welfare and mental, physical and spiritual balance of both horse and rider.

It is fundamental for us to remember that the horse is a horse and not to try to humanise him. A horse has his own nature and instincts, which look, not for a human type of love and affection but primarily for a trusted leader and friend.

In his natural environment the horse is part of a hierarchy which he both understands and respects. He will be relaxed and calm in his herd and he seeks the same way of life with us. People may seek a more stressful, high-powered existence, but we should be mindful of the true nature of the horse whilst working to fulfil our personal goals and ambitions. This path will take us to a deeper and more meaningful level of understanding, within our teaching of horses and riders.

The horse looks for a trusted leader and friend

Finding the path to empowerment

Personal empowerment for me has been a gift from the horse. I am reminded that it was in the beginning the horse who was my teacher.

Personal empowerment has been a gift from the horse

Relaxation
and focus are
fundamental
requirements
for learning

My path as a trainer has guided me to teach the importance of achieving a mental, physical and spiritual balance for both horse and rider. Relaxation and focus are fundamental requirements for learning. The rider attempts to cope with technical instruction plus communicating with another living creature. When teaching the rider, it is worth remembering to structure the lessons to facilitate this balance.

Personal empowerment from within

An awareness of our own behaviour is so important if we are to become the herd leader for the horse. He will be affected by the smallest signals from our state of mind and body language, whether we are conscious of them or not. We have the capacity to instigate either calmness or fear and qualities of either leadership or indecision. We are responsible for creating the best environment for gaining his trust, through taking time, patience and giving reward. In this way the horse will learn and gain pride in his achievement.

It is also important for the trainer to empower his pupils and riders, not only to become successful competitors but also with a fundamental understanding of responsible horsemanship. This path will ensure that both horse and rider achieve a level of confidence, harmony and ability within their training.

Human learning can become dominated by technical, analytical left-brain function, seeking achievement through the ability to make rational decisions. To understand this point for a moment, just visualise the following scene.

Imagine that you have planned to walk to the coast weighing up which small tracks to take whilst plotting a course from a map. You walk for a while, concentrating on the detail of the route you have planned. Quite suddenly, you find yourself standing at the edge of the cliffs, overlooking a view of the sun setting across the horizon. Your thoughts are transformed within an instant and become immersed in the moment. The glow of the sunset surrounds you, creating a magical aura of colour.

Thoughts of planning the route have left you completely and

you just feel a warm harmonious glow, at one with nature and the universe.

This illustration shows the capacity we have to change our mood. If we can learn to use this skill of visualisation whilst teaching and riding it will enhance our capacity for creativity and connection.

Our ability to process and analyse information is important in our communication, but it can lead to conflict where we are over-concerned about making mistakes. We may begin trying too hard to achieve and the thought process of evaluation begins with, 'am I going to succeed?' and 'will my efforts be good enough?' This thought process may be taken further as we become really fearful of making any mistakes. Thankfully, making mistakes is an important part of the journey. Mistakes give us the time to think, 'what went wrong and why didn't that work?'

My initial mistake when I was riding Delfin with strong yet totally ineffective aids became my first important step to discovery. This 'mistake' led me to question my communication skills with a highly sensitive stallion. I felt totally inadequate and angry with myself and more importantly I had felt frustration with my beautiful stallion.

From this place of turmoil the seed was planted and I became more receptive to listening and a more humble and willing pupil. I had to accept my lack of competence and realise that my more lasting and fulfilling empowerment would come from patience, acceptance, listening, and connection.

Your thoughts are transformed — you become immersed in the moment

TRYING OR ALLOWING

To gain this connection with the horse, we need to understand how we respond to a training situation and how we can deal with our self-made tension and stress. It is helpful when we understand how to utilise a balance in our pattern of thinking, which includes more understanding of what might be known as right-brain function.

Horses experience with clarity, living within the moment whereas riders come with questions, thoughts relating to past experience and much 'mind chatter' which clutters any clarity of mind. We need to develop our focus and quietness of thought, to connect with the horse – within the moment!

I spend time with riders teaching them to enhance their self-awareness and body language. This allows more creativity to flow and enhances communication, confidence and spontaneous release. The horse responds to us much more readily when we can gain this state of 'allowing and release' rather than trying too hard and blocking our natural creativity.

I have spent time as an artist and I found that if I could just 'let go' and allow creativity to flow, the picture would take on a good quality.

If however I spent too much time trying too hard to achieve 'perfection' the painting often ended up in the waste bin! We can easily stifle our natural ability, whilst trying to obtain what we conceive as 'perfection'.

Once we can grasp the idea of 'allowing' and not 'trying too hard' we can enhance our inner skills and sensitivity, intuition and

Allow creativity to flow and enhance communication

The artist has allowed creativity to flow

individual expression. If we can find our own inner harmony, we are on the path to achieving harmony with our horse.

When a trainer grasps the importance of this concept, the teaching becomes less intense, but more may be achieved. The rider who is told to have an allowing hand may find it comes more easily, from an *allowing mind*.

An allowing hand comes more easily from an allowing mind

As we acquire insight into our own behaviour, we can more meaningfully communicate with the horse and gain not only his respect, but also the greatest of friendship. Both human and horse can learn together, increasing in wisdom and insight, not only for training but also for gaining direction for life.

The horse will willingly devote himself to us and will become our greatest friend and teacher.

Many clients who spent time training with my stallions were able to return home feeling more confident to launch out on furthering their personal journey of discovery with their own horses.

Written below are extracts from some of their personal diaries of events and progress as their training continued.

Their path towards self-mastery and a closer connection with their horse may be helpful to you as you embark on your own unique way to seek further enlightenment. The first study is by Liz Smith.

Case Study by LIZ SMITH

Matrix is my second horse and my first Iberian. I came across the breed via another livery on my yard. Initially I was looking for an established horse with a good level of training that I could learn more advanced moves on.

My visit to see him was meant to be purely a fact-finding mission, having never even sat on a PRE [*Pura Raza Española* or purebred Spanish horse]. When I arrived I learned that he was only five, had arrived from Spain two weeks earlier and had just been gelded. Whilst my initial reaction was to say no, thank you and walk away. My trusted friend encouraged me to at least sit on him 'as we had driven all this way'. His stunning good looks and willing nature won me over and two weeks later he was mine.

The following two years were a real journey. In parallel to improving his schooling I worked on our relationship from the ground. However, I found lunge work a challenge as Matrix is very agile and could do a great impression of a circus stallion, rearing and spinning on his back legs and changing direction all in a split second. I couldn't react fast enough and found it hard to anticipate when he would do this. In the end I would set him off in canter on a shorter length line to get him moving forward in smaller circles, then let the line out gradually but this wasn't foolproof. However, on the ground and in the stable he respected me and would move away when I walked towards him.

Although Matrix was gelded before he came to me, he still retains many stallion characteristics. Around his stable he absolutely senses when people appear nervous and will aim to intimidate them by stamping his feet and swinging his back end out. He also tries to stand up to certain geldings and some males. However he is perfect with mares and when tacked up he's an absolute gentleman.

Whilst things had come on between Matrix and me, I felt that there was something missing and I couldn't quite get through to him on the lunge and quality free schooling was just not happening.

I'd heard Jenny's name and did some

research on the web. We corresponded by email and she felt that she could help me so I went down to meet her and her beautiful horses.

In my professional career I work at board level in business and have become used to absorbing a certain amount of pressure and having a constant amount of 'noise' in my head. This occasionally manifests itself in my body and affects my posture, and so sports massages and occasional visits to an osteopath are required. So I guess I shouldn't have been surprised that in Jenny's first session we concentrated on me and my ability to relax and breathe properly from my diaphragm. I found this a really helpful grounding and am now able to consciously put myself in this zone when needed.

My first session with Delfin wasn't very successful at all. I'll admit that I struggled to get any connection with him. But there were a couple of very small breakthroughs where I was able to ask him to vary his pace through the use of my breathing. I did however find the whole thing very emotional.

On leaving Jenny I can't honestly say that I instantly became a convert. I actually didn't try to practise anything with Matrix until the weather changed and a heavy fall of snow before Christmas meant that hacking was out of the question. And so to give Matrix a break from schooling I took him in the lunge pen and proceeded to loose school him. Well, through the use of energy and eye contact we did indeed have a breakthrough the very first time I tried Jenny's technique. I had always thought of energy as being rather passive. But now I describe it as a state of mind that translates itself into the body and comes out in, and is influenced by, posture, attitude, confidence etc. So if I want Matrix to move away from me or increase his pace, I'll walk towards him with strong eye to eye contact almost as though I am going to 'give him a piece of my mind'. I give no voice command, just a positive, erect body posture and overall purpose. The opposite is the case to slow him down. This is my interpretation of what Jenny covered in a few short hours.

Motivated by my success I tried the same technique with an ex-riding-school cob who was new to the yard and who I had not worked with before. His owner hadn't had him for long and was keen to get him to move forward; a challenge for a horse whose main role in life seemed to be conserving energy! Well it was a real transformation and I was so pleased as you can imagine.

My journey with Matrix continues but I genuinely believe that Jenny opened a door to me to gain a better understanding between my horse and me.

Free schooling is no longer a chore and there is now a 'conversation' taking place between the two of us.

The next study was written by Maggie Newman-Rose, Psychodynamic Art and Creative Psychotherapist and Life Coach and Tutor.

Case Study by MAGGIE NEWMAN-ROSE

My work as an Art and Creative Psychotherapist is rewarding and inspiring but last year I had reason to reflect on the speed of my life, and how this may be affecting my relationships; especially with my horses.

Work was becoming more evidence based and my need for visual affirmation seemed to be choking my spiritual and psychic awareness. I was stuck: still watching, still riding, but not, I subsequently realised, listening to my horses or myself. I was starting to talk to them like a foreigner abroad: louder, slower, but with impatience and a growing awareness that most of what I had learned was no longer working!

I needed an inspiration – I had valued and learned much from the many paths I had taken: studying primates, horses and humans – but I was unsure to whom I should turn.

By chance, I found Jenny's internet images of her stallions, I was captivated, and decided to read her book *Ride from the Heart*. I soon realised I had to meet a woman who seemed to have what I needed. I was sceptical though, thinking 'she may be able to do it but can I learn from her, and more importantly, what can I bring away with me?'

Within minutes of being in Jenny's company, I felt an anticipation and excitement; she seemed to want to give me as much knowledge as I could ask for. It was evident I was not there just to witness and learn from her skills but, more, I sensed I was to have something made just for me.

I was once asked about the importance of knowing when to study the 'right things' and when to dismiss the rest. I thought of the old adages 'when the pupil is ready the teacher appears' and 'talented people make everything look easy' and this was true in Jenny's case but there was something else I was yet to discover about my time with her.

I believe we are in the company of people who can dramatically change our thinking and learning patterns when we experience the thought of having prior knowledge of what they teach us. We think this, not in an arrogant way, but more like it has always been within us and we just somehow needed it to be acknowledged and retrieved.

→

As I listened to Jenny, I reflected on whether we have always had a profound and primitive awareness of how to communicate with animals but in many of us this remains unconscious, making the tools and ability to interpret their use, largely inaccessible. I sensed Jenny's skills were not only found in her dedication to training and thorough knowledge of her subject but also in her ability to convey, simply and clearly, without pretence, what we would like from our horses. She was helping to bring us to a more conscious awareness of our behaviour to help us to achieve these goals.

I watched Jenny work with her stallion and I was struck by their relationship.

My work is linked with the study of attachment patterns between people; and here in front of me, between human and horse, was the synchronicity found between mother and infant. Their bodily gestures, rhythms of questions and responses, the sometimes-silent language, were all being mirrored back and forth to each other. As adults, we know we have heard that language before, but it belonged to a time when we excluded everyone else; ➡

Jenny working with Delfin

it was a special 'speak' between Mother and us – if we were lucky it was our first communication.

I also recognised the similarity between Jenny's communication with her horse and 'Intensive Interaction', a form of pre-speech communication therapy used with young autistic children and those with learning difficulties. Jenny appeared to wait for the moment and I remembered when, as a child, I would wait before jumping into a skipping-rope game – one, two, three, jump. Could I match the speed? Could I move in time?' Jenny was changing speed and direction as she anticipated the horse's next movement and followed for a brief moment, only then to redirect him without breaking rhythm. The focus of attachment between Mother and baby is disruption and repair and I was seeing a modified version: as the horse physically chewed on a new challenge, Jenny, with her impeccable timing, was able to wait, then respond and redirect. Jenny and her

stallion were mirroring each other, they were playing, talking, and laughing – something I had forgotten how to do with my own horses.

As the day progressed, I learned about my own breathing and its role in just 'being, training and relating' to horses. I learned how to breath as a form of communication and as a method of redirecting and instructing the horse, both from mounted and ground work, I learned how to dance again, to energise and to calm and I rediscovered the language that my horses and I both understood – from this I could receive and send thoughts and wishes.

My original question as to whether Jenny and her stallions could teach me a new direction had been confirmed and the learning I gained from my time with her has changed the lives of my horses and my own. I believe Jenny has a spirit of life, which lives within her, and her ability to believe in the invisible continues to inspire me.

The final study in this chapter was written by Carolyn Jenkinson who has spent much of her life improving her skills in both natural and classical horsemanship. She used to compete in dressage (training up to medium level), and took her BHSAI and studied for the BHSII examinations. She has searched for empathic methods of training to help her to form a real and lasting partnership with her horses. Currently she has a Dutch Warmblood horse, called Jos.

Case Study by CAROLYN JENKINSON

Having returned to riding after a 25-year break I was busy re-learning all the things I used to know – trying to rediscover balance and feel and regain confidence that had definitely disappeared with age; I had bought a 16.1hh Dutch Warmblood, seven-year-old gelding called Jos, who, if truth be told, was a bit more horse than I was ready for at that point. However we were making great strides in our relationship and alongside the dressage training I had been using groundwork and natural horsemanship to build confidence and trust between us; but I was still exploring as I felt something was missing and I felt that it was to do with my ability to tune in to and truly communicate with my horse. I was enjoying looking at classical work, ridden and in hand, which is how I came across Jenny and felt that her work could be the missing piece of the jigsaw.

After avidly reading her first book and watching the video I started trying out some of her techniques and I was very impressed. I thought to myself that if my ham-fisted first tries had such a profound effect on my horse where might this journey take us both? It appeared to me that he understood what I was doing straight away and, despite being fresh and happy and full of go, he was definitely tuning in to me and reacting when I breathed out into an upward transition or in for a downward transition. It also helped me start to obtain relaxation in his gaits as he started to breath with me in trot and in canter – he let go in all the places where he usually holds tension, and so did I. I couldn't quite believe it. Another benefit that I found was that prior to using Jenny's breathing techniques I usually felt that my shoulders were sore and my muscles hurt after my rides (due to tension) but after incorporating Jenny's techniques as preparation for and during the ride the soreness was much reduced!

I also started to focus on breathing during hacking out – something I usually find quite nerve-wracking. Jos and I were building a good relationship at home but I had been letting him down when out and about as I lost my nerve for speed and kept thinking he would take off with me; so one of my goals was to overcome that problem. Whilst out I used all Jenny's breathing techniques for the whole ride and we trotted forward and fast but soft and relaxed – on a loose rein. I then just breathed in and he walked; then later I breathed out into canter and he just stayed in a rhythmic gentle canter, again on a totally loose rein. If I wanted to slow a bit I just breathed in and then breathed in again for a transition down – along with a gentle twinkle on one rein now and then – but

→

I hardly touched his mouth at all during the whole ride; just a gentle contact the whole time. It was the most fantastic feeling, he felt so relaxed, soft and connected – even with a horse thundering along behind us and then coming alongside, or going past he never got faster or stronger; it was me who 'breathed' the shots.

I have also visited Jenny a couple of times and had the joy of watching her work with her stallions first hand. I had also been given the opportunity to practise some in-hand work with her stallion Maestu and to gain some tuition from Jenny whilst riding Maestu on the lunge line, which meant I could concentrate on my breathing and the effect it was having on this magical and thoughtful stallion.

Since these visits I have incorporated the breathing and centring when leading, tacking up and handling Jos and also during ground and in-hand work. I am finding it helps in all sorts of situations: to bond us together, create focus and calm and to soothe him (and me!) In fact there are lots of occasions when I am very thankful for having discovered this way of connecting with my horse. For example on one occasion he was very fresh and distracted in a show atmosphere in the warm-up ring. Again I focused on all the breathing techniques I had learned blending them with lateral work and transitions, and was able to get Jos to relax, lower his head and stretch. He was able to listen to me and mirror my relaxation, becoming much calmer and safe to ride.

I find too that ensuring I am using Jenny's techniques when teaching Jos new things helps keep him calm and relaxed, which means he is in the right frame of mind to learn. It also has fun connotations; I use it when learning to do liberty work or playing with Jos in his field or the arena as I find it really helps me in lowering or raising his energy or moving up or down through gaits.

It makes our relationship more beautiful, it enables us both to get the best out of each other in whatever we are doing or learning and is becoming an intrinsic part of who and what we are.

Both human and horse can learn together

Both human and horse can learn together, increasing in wisdom and insight, not only for training but also for gaining direction for life.

Chapter 3

Breathe into Natural Posture and Balance

> When we sit on the back of the horse, we connect with true nature and move as one
>
> — JENNY ROLFE

Thoughts and insights

My love for horses together with a deep admiration for the classical tradition of riding has led me to travel to several countries to gain valuable insight and experience. My journey has meant that I have questioned many of my initial values and concepts.

There is a maze of techniques which are available to us as tools to help us train the horse. This quest can end up in confusion if you only emulate the technique of other Masters. Much time can be spent in perfecting your technique, but to really connect with the essence of the horse, you need to experience a greater gift. If you seek to become your own Master, this will help you to gain self-belief as you create your own unique path on the road of horsemanship. I understand more fully now that anything of real value has to come from the heart and soul. You have to feel

Seek to become your own master

it from a deeper level, which helps to create your own authority, intuition and wisdom.

As my experience grew, I began to understand the value of personal empowerment and listening to my own intuition and sense of feel. These were the greatest lessons for me having spent many hours absorbing the teachings of some exceptionally skilled trainers and horsemen. For many years I have spent endless hours of quiet time, both riding and just being together with my stallions. A background of music creates the ambience for focus, meditation and creativity, which has become a shared experience for me and my horses.

The more I tuned into my horse and his movement, the more I discovered how the depth of my breathing created an immediate response from the horse. This state of mind together with a focus on core breathing can be the essence for a truly balanced rider position and effective, mobilised seat.

Core breathing is the essence for a balanced rider
....

Looking at lifestyle

Let us look at how we can change our approach to our normal daily tasks to become more conscious of ourselves mentally and physically. This sensitivity will prove the key to our communication with the horse. You may not be aware of it, but from the time you are awake in the morning you will be using your hands to control and connect with your environment.

Just spend a few moments to think about how much you rely on using your arms and hands. They are instrumental when preparing meals and in most of the daily chores. Without using your hands, everyday tasks such as driving a car or answering a telephone would become extremely difficult. Arms and hands play a fundamental part of every activity within a busy lifestyle. You may, for example, observe a person who is full of anger or frustration just waving his arms in dismay or shaking his fist with anger.

Balance is often assisted by using your hands. For instance as you walk down a staircase, or a ladder, you may use your hands to gain more stability.

So, with these concepts in mind it can be quite difficult to change our attitude when we are sitting on the back of a horse. It may come more naturally to take up a contact with the reins before we have even thought of establishing our own link with our seat and core. Through much of our lives we are not consciously connected with our core or our breathing. Often we are not aware of our body unless we are feeling some pain or discomfort.

Connect with your emotions

When you see a person laughing do you just look at the mouth or the 'smile' from their eyes? Emotions are initially experienced in the core and if you just start to laugh out loud, you will feel a vibration through your abdomen. The laugh is immediately felt within your core.

Imagine a very distressing scene where you are touched by deep sadness which brings you close to tears. The emotion vibrates within your core before the tears come. We are told that emotions such as anger are harboured in our liver and spleen which can over time create illness and blocked energy within the body.

It becomes more obvious that if we can be in tune with our core then we are connected with our emotions. The practice of

> Look for the smile from their eyes

core breathing techniques will gradually assist our emotional balance and help us to live and ride with greater harmony and self-awareness.

Regular practice of core breathing will not only help us in our riding but will also enhance our health, strength and energy, whatever our age.

As techniques of breathing help to unlock the clutter of unresolved emotions and fears, the body will respond with greater fluidity. Tension creates restriction and deeper breathing can release the energy that is blocked, so the rider can absorb the movement of the horse and create a flow of harmony.

Below is a case study written by Linda who brought her Appaloosa stallion Luca to my yard for training.

Case Study | LINDA AND LUCA, APPALOOSA

Spring – summer 2009

Luca was difficult to lead from the field: barging and pushing and generally badly behaved on his head collar. I was worried about riding him as he used to rear and I had fallen off. He was also scary out hacking, over-zealous at shows, and he reared and was badly behaved on the lunge. If I am honest, I was a little frightened of him.

Winter 2009

In the winter of 2009, Luca was turned away in the hope he would behave himself in the spring but it didn't happen! In January 2010 I read Jenny's article in the British Dressage magazine and thought that her clinic could be the help I needed. I was keen to go to the clinic as I had run out of ideas on how to manage Luca and was afraid of losing control of him altogether.

March 2010 – visit to Jenny's clinic

The clinic was very enlightening and I picked up just a flavour of Jenny's knowledge and what she had to offer. I tried practising the core breathing but found it very difficult to find the muscles and use them correctly. The breathing techniques did calm Luca somewhat but I was still not happy with my ability to manage my body language.

→

June 2010 – I returned to Devon with Luca to get one-to-one help.
It soon became obvious that my anxious, up-tight and loud behaviour upset Luca profoundly. I had made the big mistake of humanising Luca. Jenny said 'A horse does not want to be kissed and cuddled; he needs a calm place to be!!' I learnt a lot in those few days about myself. If I wanted the best from Luca I had to make a lot of changes, take my time and think before I did things instead of jumping straight in with both feet, rushing about like a headless chicken.

On my return home from Devon, I started on my journey with Luca to be assertive but calm. In the early days I would try too hard and fast to get Luca working in a 'shape'. Luca would respond with, 'I am not doing that!' and Jenny's words 'less is more' popped into my head and I allowed more. When I am tense I remember Jenny's words 'Relax, breathe from your core, imagine you are wearing your favourite slippers.'

Out hacking I asked Luca to halt to let a car pass by (he doesn't like waiting); I thought I was relaxed and tried to calm him, but as the car past by I saw another car but Luca was ready to go. To stop him I became tense and realised it was the wrong thing to do. To calm him, I then tried to relax totally and kept still, but the totally relaxed state I put myself in made me feel completely out of my 'comfort zone' and vulnerable. All this time, I thought I had been relaxed and yet I still had a long way to go.

Linda offers Luca a calm place of leadership

The New Year of 2011

Trying to relax absolutely and breathe through my core whilst riding is still a task for me.

In loose work we walk, trot and canter, and some lateral movements are fuelled by my core breathing and Luca's intuition and willingness to be led by me. We are firm partners now and have lots of fun hacking out. There is still some tension when we warm up at a show, however; I have discovered that I still hold a lot of tension because other riders close to me seem to bother me and this makes Luca tense.

Everything Luca does on the ground is led by my actions. I am still trying to change a lifetime of being uptight and tense to becoming a calmer being.

I will continue to keep a diary of events for my lifetime with Luca. This is my passion, enlightenment and a great place to just BE.

An effective position and seat comes from deep within

The position and seat of the rider will become more effective when we study the individual person, not only the outer form and position, but the mind and focus of the rider from deep within.

In this context, the word 'position' should imply stillness, i.e. calmness and stability, but not immobility.

Within training we will be asking the horse to move through active limbs and joints into a fluid spine capable of release and contraction within the motion.

If the rider is to become the image for the horse to follow then he also needs to allow release and contraction within his spine. Core breathing allows energy to flow as a wave in the sea, which draws power inwards and then releases energy outwards.

My search for the truth within horsemanship has shown me that when we sit on the back of the horse and feel love and empathy with his nature, this can be the first important note, allowing the symphony to begin.

A place that feels like home for the soul of the horseman

The musician will leave the world behind as his mind feels a sense of freedom, enhanced by the moving experience of the music. He will feel such joy, which leaves behind the problems of the world giving only clarity and freedom of spirit and expression, within that moment. This is also a place that feels like home for the soul of the horseman.

Core breathing allows energy to flow as a wave in the sea

Creating self-awareness

I believe the essence of training for the rider begins on the ground. In this way the rider can begin to understand the influence of both posture and core breathing.

Core breathing is a very potent tool which can help us to focus with clarity and be within the moment. In this way the mind will slow down and we can find more simplicity in our thoughts as we focus with intent in that moment of time. This will be our important place for connection with the mind and spirit of the horse.

Our minds will not be cluttered and dulled by the stress of problems from yesterday; neither will we be concerned about the problems to be tackled tomorrow. All our focus will be within that moment to 'feel' the enhanced connection of body, mind and spirit, ready to connect with the horse.

Find simplicity in your thoughts

The horse is very responsive and will quickly sense a quietness of spirit. If we can provide him with a place of trust and calm then we can build on this connection to gain a deep friendship with the horse. He will become the 'mirror of our mind'.

Before we delve into techniques to enhance body awareness, try this simple exercise which demonstrates the importance of your breathing.

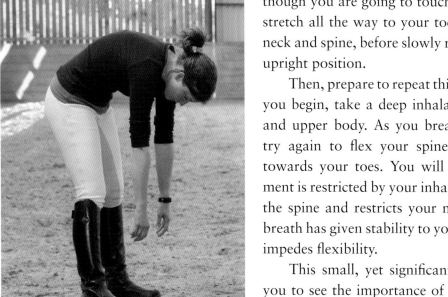

Lean forwards as though you are going to touch your toes

Standing in good posture, lean forwards, as though you are going to touch your toes but don't stretch all the way to your toes. Relax your head, neck and spine, before slowly returning to a normal upright position.

Then, prepare to repeat this exercise but, before you begin, take a deep inhalation into your chest and upper body. As you breathe deeply inwards, try again to flex your spine forwards, reaching towards your toes. You will find that the movement is restricted by your inhalation which tightens the spine and restricts your mobility. The inward breath has given stability to your upper body which impedes flexibility.

This small, yet significant, exercise may help you to see the importance of breathing awareness and how this can influence your body when riding.

The body can lock tension in any of the joints, for instance a clenched hand will create tightness within the arm and shoulder and may restrict mobility within the back. We can learn so much about ourselves and where we lock tension, by spending valuable time without the horse to just connect with our own body, whilst on the ground.

Further exercises to enhance self-awareness

These exercises will help you to become more conscious of how easily tension can restrict mobility when riding. Also they show how we can influence and support our core through a focus on breathing.

EXERCISE 1 – FOCUS ON BREATHING

Stand normally in the basic **top-to-toe** position (see page 92) and try this simple exercise. Walk forward with your hands on your hips and breathe deeply into your stomach and follow with a deep exhalation. Can you feel the swing and release within your hips and more freedom within your arms as you exhale?

Follow this by taking a deep breath inwards and continue with more shallow breathing. Much of the release and mobilisation disappears.

You will find that the deep inhalation will block your forward movement as the spine strengthens and lengthens. This is the power of our breathing. It can either enhance mobility or create stilted movement.

EXERCISE 2 – BREATHING TO ASSIST MOBILISATION

A further exercise is to stand tall and really arch your back, placing your hands on your hips. Bring your sternum (breast bone) both up and out. Then take a deep inward breath.

Now, with hands on hips, try to mobilise your seat and pelvis both backwards and forwards. You will find that your arched back tightens your spine which will restrict fluidity when you are riding. Our aim is for good balanced posture as fully described in my **top-to-toe** posture for the rider (see page 92). We need to be aware of the mobility within our pelvis and core muscles. Tightness within our shoulders and spine can restrict core mobility. For the rider this means that the seat cannot release and flow naturally with the motion of the horse. When we build core awareness we are creating an effective connection with the horse so that we can more readily, influence his movement whilst maintaining fluidity within our core. If we can ride whilst maintaining a 'neutral' seat or core, it will be useful when we wish to either instigate

*F*ocus on your breathing

A tight arched spine will block movement of the core

energy or to rebalance and steady, as with a half-halt. A neutral seat allows mobility within the core to connect with the movement of the horse. From this centre of balance we can either influence with more core energy to energise the horse or we can steady and rebalance with a deeper stabilising inward breath.

EXERCISE 3 – CORE (SEAT) MOBILITY

Before performing this exercise for core mobility, just try standing in the basic position used for the top-to-toe posture for the rider.

Push your weight down into your heel – bringing your toe upwards. Now place your hand on your inner thigh and feel the tightness through your whole leg. When we overstretch and tighten any of our joints and muscles, this will be mirrored throughout our body.

When the rider's legs are overstretched and become tight, it is impossible for the core muscles to release a more mobilised seat. Now you will become more aware of how easily your seat can be blocked by tension in other parts of the body.

Now let us look at this circular core stretch exercise to help mobilise the core muscles.

1. Stand in a basic position (see page 92) for relaxation with your feet parallel and shoulder width apart. Sink your weight into your knees and ankles.

2. Imagine there is a clock face inscribed in a large circle around your pelvis. Take a deep inward breath and release your core muscles forwards with the outward breath, as if sitting on a swing and pushing it forwards. This will tilt your pelvis towards 12 at the top of the clock.

3. Release from the waist, allowing your core muscles to stretch to the right side at 3; enjoy the sideways stretch.

4. Relax and lengthen your muscles from your waist into your lower back. Imagine you are about to sit on a chair behind you. Just release your knees and allow your seat to stretch backwards and lower – towards 6 on the clock.

5. Allow the core muscles to slowly swing towards the left – 9 on the clock. Start to enjoy the flexibility and use your core muscles to rotate your pelvis and gently mobilise around these points on the clock.

6. Practise this exercise slowly in both directions – you may feel it is much easier in one direction but for riding, this core mobility will be beneficial in helping to influence the horse.

This exercise will assist core mobility and help to make you consciously connected to your core.

EXERCISE 4 – FOR TENSION IN THE ARMS

Clench your left fist very tightly. Now use your right hand to stroke your left arm gently, starting with your hand, up through your arm and towards your shoulder blades. Notice how the tightness of a clenched fist causes restriction all the way up your arm to your shoulder.

Wherever we carry tightness and tension, we will create a block of resistance within our body. This will prevent the flow of energy required to enable us to perform and move with fluidity. If we cannot allow this release of energy and power then we will not be capable of absorbing the energetic movement of the horse.

When we sit on the back of the horse we are looking not only for a connection of minds but also a connection between two living beings striving to move together in balance and harmony.

Understanding balance – the key to harmony

So what do we mean by riding in balance and harmony and why is this so important?

Do you ever watch the ice skating on television? It is interesting to observe the more professional skaters who have learnt to move with fluidity, grounded core energy and balance. Less experienced skaters are not so grounded and connected and this

Balance and
harmony
·················

creates more tension through their limbs, hence they lose their
balance more easily.

Deeper core breathing helps to create both stability and
mobility. To sit like a puppet seeking the perfect position will not
be very productive. We need balance and poise but not in a fixed
position. With every stride taken by the horse, we will be making
slight adjustments so that we can synchronise with his movement
and power.

If we can develop a natural self-carriage and posture based on
self-awareness and core-breathing techniques, it will make it easier
for the horse to carry the weight of a rider in a good balance. At a
deeper level if we are in tune with our emotions and feelings then
we will be in a balanced place to connect and listen to the horse.
This requires a real awareness of posture and core breathing which

will enable us to synchronise with the movement of the horse. Lessons on the lunge can be very helpful as the rider can spend time 'feeling' the movement with focus on core breathing. Time spent on the lunge can help the rider to learn how to influence the balance of the horse. It gives him the opportunity to focus solely on himself and to take the time to just 'be', 'allow' and 'connect'.

It is extremely important for us to feel stability and balance, and so it is essential to have a correctly fitted saddle that sits well on the horse. This will help the rider to achieve a good, balanced position.

The horse moves with a swinging backward and forward motion, plus uphill elevation, with each stride, within each gait. His ribcage will also naturally swing from side to side. The rider has to absorb all this movement to gain security in the saddle or he will just bounce heavily, becoming totally unstable within the movement.

The following exercise using steps or stairs can help us to understand how we absorb our own movement whilst on foot.

Begin by walking along level ground, then place your foot on the first step or stair and feel the elevation needed through the upper torso for the uphill movement. Can you feel the lift in your upper body as you bring your foot up to the next step? If you do not lift forward and upwards, through your core and upper torso, you will block the upward step.

When riding we need to think not only of forward riding but also of absorbing the upward motion and elevation of the movement. As we become more aware of this, it will be easier to maintain fluidity and balance as the motion is more efficiently absorbed.

If we allow our shoulders to flow with the movement, rather than riding with a fixed spine and shoulders, we can move more freely with the shoulders of the horse.

> Take the time to just 'be', 'allow' and 'connect'

Place your foot on the step and feel the elevation through the upper torso

When the shoulders become fixed, the restriction extends through the spine and arms of the rider, and so it is impossible for energy to flow through the spine and upper torso. Relaxed lowered shoulders sustained by deeper core breathing will allow both expansion and release through the upper body.

We have looked at a lifestyle that focuses on our arms and hands which, when we get into the saddle, may still influence us to put too much energy into strong arms rather than a powerful, balanced seat and core. It is, therefore, helpful to ride with the reins in one hand just for a few minutes, thus encouraging a focus of feel and balance within the body, which is not impeded by any stiffness within the arms. This gives the rider some time to relax with the horse and allow his body posture to mirror the horse's motion.

A rider may appear to be in a good position with an erect posture and elevated chest but if the spine is not supported by correct breathing then the back becomes weak and hollow, which the horse will then mirror within his movement.

Ride with the reins in one hand to encourage a natural body flow
....

Core connection

My connection with the horse is through an awareness of energy created through breathing. The inward breath takes in air which will energise and give life force to the body. The outward breath is a release of air, excess energy and stress. Look at the ocean waves and the way energy is harnessed as the wave draws in energy and then unleashes it with force. Using a similar basic principle we can utilise energy from the power of the breath to control both ourselves and the horse.

Imagine making a huge releasing sigh then just allowing the inward breath to happen in a natural way. Tension just begins to disappear. On the next outward breath, feel as if the tension is flowing down your torso and relaxing your spine. Take an inward breath, filling upwards and expanding the ribcage wide and full to support your upper body and release tightness between your shoulder blades. This allows your shoulders to move more easily with your horse.

The key to fluidity within riding is to understand how to use the seat and core muscles to assist freedom and mobility to move with the motion of the horse. When we learn how to instigate movement from our core, we give our upper body more stability. This allows our legs to relax, lengthen and hang down freely either side of the ribcage of the horse.

Most of us spend more time using our body from the shoulders upwards. We are often busy talking and, less frequently, listening. Our eyes are constantly observing our surroundings. Our minds can become overactive with a continuous stream of thoughts that will affect us on a physical level. Our head and cranium will tighten which restricts blood flow and freedom of movement. The neck will also become restricted and tight, causing tightness within our shoulder blades and upper torso.

The aim of focusing on core breathing will be to calm the mind, release the tension and create a flow of energy through our core muscles and seat.

Harness energy as a wave in the sea

This makes perfect sense for the rider, as physically we make contact through our core muscles, which control the connection through our seat.

When teaching riders, much of my time is spent looking at posture and body awareness using exercises from the ground. If the rider seeks to really advance his skills, then time given to focusing on poise, breathing and posture from the ground will prove to be an invaluable golden tool.

If we regularly use exercises to enhance our self-awareness, the time spent on the back of the horse will become more fruitful. We can exert far more influence upon the mind of the horse when we experience harmony of our body, mind and spirit. The effective rider will not be the person who learns only to sit correctly but the individual who understands how to truly connect using deeper senses from within.

It is interesting to watch a person running using regular, deep breathing because this enables him to maintain a steady rhythm and energy within each stride. Every athlete can enhance performance, both mentally and physically, by using steady, deep and rhythmic core breathing. Unlike the athlete, a rider has to focus not only on personal balance and energy but also upon another sensitive, highly energetic living creature – the horse!

Focus on poise, breathing and posture

'Top to toe' postural awareness

You will find it helpful to practise the following postural techniques and exercises. They will show you quite graphically how breathing can support the essence of good posture and have a profound influence on your whole body.

Basic position

Let us begin with a **basic position** that will enhance stability, balance and poise. These techniques are similar to the ancient wisdoms of the east, such as Chi Gong and Tai Chi. As I study the power of breathing, I realise that my personal journey has taken me on a similar path to the teaching of martial artists and Eastern philosophers.

Find a quiet place where you will not be disturbed and if possible play some soothing, relaxing music whilst you go through these techniques below.

Basic position

- Stand quietly and cultivate the feeling of breathing into the space around you. Now make a slow, deep outward sigh.

- Your feet should be parallel, about shoulder width apart and facing towards the front (neither turned in or out). Focus on your feet and push your weight down, first into your toes and then into your heels, resting finally with your feet equally weighted on the ground. Have a feeling of connecting through your legs and feet, into the core of the earth – 'feeling truly grounded'. (You can practise with flat comfortable shoes or bare feet.)

- Relax down through your legs, into released knees and ankles as if you are skiing down a bumpy slope and absorbing the irregular bumps.

- Grow taller and expand your posture allowing your head to come slightly forward and upwards. Do not tighten the back of the neck but allow it to lengthen, keeping a relaxed jaw.

- Cultivate the feeling that your head is balanced in lightness, floating above the shoulders, like a balloon above your body. This lengthening of the neck helps to release the shoulders.

- Soften the muscles around your eyes. Focus and stare straight ahead at a single object and then immediately relax into 180 degree softer vision, taking in the whole vista.

- Relax the facial muscles and release the jaw. If you push your tongue into the roof of your mouth, just for a few moments, this will help you to soften your jaw. Allow the back of your neck to lengthen gently. Relax your jaw and push back gently

Make a deep outward sigh – connect with the universe – feel truly grounded into the back of your lengthened neck. Then release into a comfortable position. This movement will help to re-align the whole of your spine.

- Keep a soft feel in your sternum whilst breathing. Expand the chest, not by tightening the sternum and hollowing your back, but by expanding through the ribcage and breathing wide and full, into your spine and between your shoulder blades.

- Make a deep outward sigh and allow the breath to ripple through your torso down into your core and through your legs and feet.

- You should start to feel more relaxed and grounded. Focus on your body awareness from your head down through to your toes.

- Become aware of breathing from your core. Expand your abdomen with your inhalation; breathe into your body – as if filling up a glass with water – from the core upwards.

- Exhale deeply down through your upper body and spine, releasing through your core. Slowly empty the glass of water! Empty the body of air from top to bottom.

Exercises to release tension in the arms

- If you can feel any tension in your shoulders just swing your arms around, away from your body. Swing with floppy arms from left to right, with energetic movements.

- Swing your arms to connect with your lower back. Allow your arms to feel like wet rags and thump gently onto your lower back as you turn. After a minute or so, slow the energy and come back to standing still.

- Bring your arms around to the front of you. Reach out as far as you can in front of your chest and imagine you are hugging a tree! Stretch your arms out as far as you can in a circle; hold them to the front of you, stretching through the outside of the arm, stretching and relaxing your wrists and fingers.

- Allow a few moments to enjoy the stretch, then bring your arms and hands down slowly by your side. Enjoy the release from your shoulders and the looseness and freedom within your arms.

above left
Swing your arms around, away from your body

....

above right
Imagine you are hugging a tree

....

Exercises for core mobility

- Begin by walking and becoming aware of your core and your breathing. Feel the release of the core as you breathe outwards more deeply. You will feel the ripple of energy down your spine. You may find it helpful to place your hand on your lower back to feel this release. This is the movement which creates a release of your core when you are riding. The horse learns quickly to respond with an upward transition or just more energy. If you sit on a swing and push it forward, this movement will give you a similar feel but, when on a horse, the feel should be far more subtle.

- Now take a really strong inward breath. This will expand your upper body and stabilise your spine. This action will naturally encourage you to stop and rebalance. This will be the essence of your half-halt when you are riding. When you inhale deeply, this will also strengthen and lengthen your inner thigh which will tell the horse to slow down as he will find it more difficult to move freely forward.

- It is of value to spend time on the ground, coordinating walking and breathing. Try to keep your breathing in a natural deeper rhythm to blend with your strides. I don't mean you should count out your breaths to match the strides but to allow a natural energy flow and not force it. The problem is that often we impede our natural breath flow because of tension. This **top-to-toe** awareness is just to help us connect again with our natural, calm state of mind. Often we are not aware of how shallow our breathing has become. If we can spend time connecting with our natural rhythm and more relaxed, deeper breathing, tension will begin to melt away.

- Use the deeper inward breath to rebalance and deeper outward breath to increase energy and mobility. Begin to develop a feel for your breathing to influence both your energy flow and stability. When you can master and control your own body you will become more influential as an effective and balanced rider.

Master your own body and master the horse

- Now place your hands on your hip bones and feel the movement whilst you are walking. Begin to synchronise your breathing within a slow rhythm. Try walking on a circle and walking laterally, feel how your core mobilises and flows in each direction. Notice how your breathing can enhance your core mobility and observe when you feel more 'stuck' in your core. You will need to keep walking with your weight down into relaxed knees and ankles for these exercises to be effective as the release through your knees allows your core to be mobile. This is a similar feel to riding. Just maintain the **basic position** described above before you begin to move forward.

- Here is a further technique to help with your awareness of lightness and self-carriage. Slump right down into your waist with your upper body and notice how your walking is restricted. Then begin to move in self-carriage – imagine walking up a step and allow the elevation within your upper body to support this movement. Feel how you can support your upper body, maintaining fluidity and poise within a natural self-carriage. Learn how to become the image for your horse to mirror.

Time spent practising these techniques will help you to become aware of tightness in your body. Over many years, you may have held tension in a particular part of your body. This may be the result of surgery, previous injury, posture at work or just general bad posture which has built up over a period time. It is amazing how 'unaware' we can be of our body in our normal, everyday life. This is a good opportunity to reflect and focus on personal equilibrium, poise and balance which will support a more healthy body and a calm mind.

Become the image for your horse to mirror

Exercise for core stability

Once we have learnt to sit in good posture and balance, we need to try to maintain this even if the horse attempts to become strong and forge ahead. If you just pull back strongly with your hands, the horse may well use his physical power against you. Once you try to control the horse through a harsh contact with his mouth, all harmony will be lost and both rider and horse will become tense and agitated.

I have a good exercise, performed from the ground, which demonstrates the power of core breathing to rebalance the horse and prevent him running way from the balance you seek.

- Have two people standing facing each other. Both will hold the reins; one person will be the 'rider', holding one end of the reins, and the other will hold the other end of the reins and be the 'horse'. The rider will stand in the relaxed **basic position**: weight down into the knees and ankles whilst supporting his posture with core breathing. The person acting as the horse will give a few small tugs on the reins which may well cause the rider to lose balance and fall forward.

- The rider then takes a deep inward breath which stabilises the core and creates strength and lengthening of the spine. Whilst the rider is breathing more deeply inwards, the horse then repeats the few small jerks on the reins. The rider will start to feel more stability and not be pulled off balance by the horse. Take a few minutes to develop this exercise as you can learn more about your own breathing and self-control and how you will affect the horse once you are sitting in the saddle.

Exercise from the ground. *above* When stability is not from the core you will lose balance

above right The deep inward breath creates core stability and strength: the essence of the half-halt

This significant exercise demonstrates that, when we are riding, if the horse is dominant and tries to forge ahead, the rider can take a strong deep breath inwards to steady and rebalance the movement. The rider can close the fingers on the reins until the horse responds by slowing the pace, allowing more weight to be supported by the hind limbs. Immediately the horse responds, the fingers are lightened on the reins so that the horse may relax again within his mouth, head and neck. Continue to ride forwards with steady rhythmic breathing.

The deep inward breath creates core strength and stability for the rider, this is the essence of the half-halt

The horse – our mirror

The horse will be our greatest teacher and he will reflect our mood, poise and self-carriage. The rider who is focused and self-aware, tuning into the nature of the horse, will be able to produce true empathy. The rider's greatest gifts are a love for the horse and a respect for his nature.

The rider can then seek to balance with a sense of feel and allowing, both mentally and physically. Time, patience and practice will reap great rewards. If you don't achieve your goals in a training session, there is always another day. We need to understand the importance of **time and patience** and not only with the horse; we can also be gentle on ourselves within our training and discipline. Many people have high aspirations to perform, always seeking perfection. Confidence may wane as riders may not fulfil their high ideals.

> The rider's greatest gifts are a love and respect for the horse

The horse is our mirror

Allow yourself time to learn lessons and time to make your mistakes. Progress will happen slowly and as it evolves, it will encompass all these goals. When the dedicated rider gives sufficient time for regular practice, these disciplines will not only assist with riding but can become lessons for life.

If you can discipline yourself to become more focused on your personal **top-to-toe** posture (see page 92) and breathing awareness, you will be in a peaceful place, where your horse can relax and be within his comfort zone. This would be similar to life in the herd, when there is no predator to disturb him and no cause for concern. The herd would be together grazing, ambling or resting, feeling secure with their natural family. All horses are totally aware of each other and their body language, as they will always be aware of our body language and state of mind.

When you open the door of the stable, take to the horse the calm focus you feel when you practise the **basic position** described in the **top-to-toe** section of this chapter.

From the first moment you are with your horse, give him this place of composure and tranquility and very soon he will become the mirror of your mind.

This will be reflected in your riding and become a sound path on which to build friendship and harmony – the essence of horsemanship.

Top to toe – quick tips for the rider

Sigh deeply to relax whole body

Begin breathing from the core

Expand and lengthen upper body

Tune into core mobility

Lengthen neck, relax jaw

Relax arms and hands

Allow weight into knees

'Carpet slipper' feet

The **initial** aid is always from your core

Listen to your horse

Free your mind to enjoy each moment

Chapter 4

Subtle Energy of Core Breathing

> The breath is the essence of all life and connection
>
> — JENNY ROLFE

The power of energy

We live in an era where the natural forces of our planet, such as the wind and the waves, are being harnessed to produce much needed energy. This will create power for the future as our modern lifestyle is rapidly destroying the natural resources of our planet.

All life is energy and if we become more aware of how our personal energy can be used to connect with the horse, a much deeper empathy can be built over a period of time. Much of our present-day teaching relates to technical knowledge but my experience, working daily with my stallions, has taught me the significance of a further dimension. The power of breathing and energy exchange remains almost unexplored between people and horses. This dimension offers a future of revelation for the student who becomes conscious of personal breathing patterns and energy.

All life is energy

When we are aware of our thoughts, body language and breathing we can communicate with the horse in a most profound way connecting with *his* world. Our busy over-active thoughts will become more tranquil as we connect with the here and now and allow the mind just to stay in the present moment. In this way we learn the personal power of just feeling, being and allowing. We can let go of our more stressful thoughts of achieving, perfecting and the demanding expectations of our normal lifestyle.

Modern society demands good verbal skills and technical knowledge to become successful, thus creating an affluent lifestyle. This type of pressure can start to create physical problems which will manifest as tension throughout our body. This can begin from tightness in our head, neck and shoulders which creates restriction through the whole spine. Our natural flow of energy is thus curbed which is the precursor to ill health.

When we become physically tight through stressful living, the natural ebb and flow of each breath becomes restricted. Life-giving oxygen cannot circulate easily through tight muscles and ligaments. Living cells become deprived of life-giving nutrients and toxins abound causing physical damage. Over a period of time energy flow becomes blocked and disturbed which will lead to ill health and personal imbalance.

Just to demonstrate these concepts, let us look at my client Susan, a student who came here to develop her connection with her young Spanish gelding. I soon sensed that her mind and thoughts were similar to an express train speeding along the track. I asked her to try to visualise cycling in the countryside on a sunny day, imagining flowers, fields, trees and the sound of birdsong.

These thoughts would help her mind to relax as she had been holding the heightened tension needed to drive a sports car at high speed.

Susan held a responsible position within a well-known company and appeared highly motivated and intelligent. We spent some time talking about self-awareness, deeper breathing and looking at exercises to help with relaxation.

Slowly, Susan began to slow her thoughts and focus within the moment. She was gaining more connection with her own body

> Every breath has a natural ebb and flow

and mind. She then began her training in the saddle and the inner focus she had gained began to shine through. Her calmer state of mind enabled her to make positive changes for herself, within her riding. For instance, Susan was rather tense in her knee and upper thigh which restricted the mobility within her seat. I was about to mention this when she became conscious of her tension. She sighed deeply, releasing through her core to relax her leg. Susan was becoming her own teacher.

Many riders are subjected to pressure and stress caused by our modern way of life and when the time comes to ride and communicate with the horse, all they have to offer is an uptight mind and a tense body that the horse will be quick to mirror.

Within Eastern culture, controlled energy is known as **chi** energy, which can be used as a vehicle for healing and also within the martial arts. In China there is an old saying: 'Where the mind goes, the chi will follow.'

Visualise flowers, fields and trees

Where the mind goes, the chi will follow

This chi energy can have a huge impact on our relationships and often when we feel on the same wavelength with another, it is created by a connection of chi.

Chi energy can be used to enhance healing normally through a state of meditation allowing the healing energy to flow through the hands and finger tips. It is good to remember these possibilities as we caress the neck of the horse to help him to become calm and release tension. If we are capable of healing and giving out therapeutic energy, the horse will immediately receive this and it can become part of our day-to-day relationship with him. This type of energy awareness will help to build a very deep bond of security and connection. We can use the power of a gentle touch to settle a horse who has suffered either physically or mentally.

Once we make a decision to take the time to focus on our breathing we become empowered to create an environment where we can flourish mentally, physically and spiritually. This decision will detach us from the pull of past events and the concern for

The power of a gentle touch

the future. We can become aware of the present moment and how we feel physically as we reconnect with our inner spirit. If we allow ourselves time to connect in this way, we can feel a depth of harmony and oneness with creation. The horse will instantly feel an attraction as we create a place for focus and communication. The connection is similar to a meditation, a communion of souls. The gulf between man and horse is bridged as all our senses are brought into that one moment in time. The horse feels our complete focus and energy as our true personality can flourish. We are not suppressed by concerns for either the past or the future.

Subtle energy

When we are in good general health, there will be an invisible aura of energy which surrounds every living creature, including human life. Much scientific evidence now recognises the importance of personal energy in the western world. For centuries the cultures of the east have placed more importance on the practice of deeper breathing to expand personal energy to support good health.

Over many years I have been fascinated to see the potent effect of our breathing upon the mind of the horse. My stallions have taught me the power of this subtle energy but I have also spent time reading books to gain enlightenment on why and how these techniques gain such profound results. I have learnt that our thoughts and emotions influence the energy signals from our heart, which can actually be felt several feet away. The expressions 'good vibes' and 'bad vibes' stem from our ability to receive energy vibrations which mirror the emotions of a person. We are all capable of receiving and transmitting subtle energy exchange, which can occur between all living beings. I believe horses are very highly tuned to receiving such signals, which could in fact save their life in a natural environment. The fear and flight instinct is based upon these signals together with a keen awareness of body language in the herd. Horses will respond immediately to any variation within their energy field as they are highly sensitive

> Our breathing has a potent effect on the mind of a horse

Fear is a deep-rooted emotion

to any change, however subtle. This explains why the awareness of our breathing to connect with the horses, can gain such amazing results. Awareness of changes in breathing and emotions *is* the language of the herd. I have heard people say that horses do not experience emotions yet they are motivated by fear and flight. Fear is a deep-rooted emotion.

My experience has taught me that the horse has a heightened awareness of our emotions which often exceeds the experience of humans. The whole universe is connected by energy. Life is energy.

Delfin, my ex-bullfighting Spanish stallion has a huge energy field which is hard to measure. A practitioner of the Bowen technique tried to calculate his energy field by dowsing and his field of energy proved immeasurable.

We all have a personal field of energy which will interact with all living creatures within its field. For example when a horse is standing several metres away from me, if I direct my thoughts, energy and focus towards his hind leg, he will feel the energy from my deeper exhalation and quietly move his leg forward.

Imagine you are walking into a stable feeling anxious or angry. You will already be sending strong energy signals to the horse that will trigger his own fear. With no conscious thought at all, messages of apprehension and distress have been conveyed to the horse. Horses flourish in a calm peaceful atmosphere where they feel secure and can interact with other horses as a herd.

Each day, as I walk into my school, a number of things contribute to a feeling of relaxation and restoration: I hear the familiar sound of chomping of hay, the stallions greet me, all calm yet alert to their environment. Classical music gives a gentle ambience to enhance this feeling. It has become a habit for me to take a huge sigh before I walk in the school. This helps me to focus on deeper core breathing which helps to calm my mind and

> Awareness of changes in breathing and emotion *is* the language of the herd

clarify my thoughts. To become conscious of our breathing is the key to understanding the language of the horse. In this way we will become part of the comfortable energy zone where the horse will find a connection. This is the beginning of a journey of discovery – to connect through our breathing.

Horses flourish in a calm atmosphere where they can interact as a herd

Building our self-awareness

When we can master our thoughts, breathing and state of mind then we will begin to feel we are living within the moment. This is the key to unlocking all of our normal, everyday defences. Suppressed fear will change to a positive focus and locked up emotions will be released as we learn to feel more comfortable in mind, body and spirit.

So let us look at why it is so important to the horse that we learn how to just 'be' and to let go of our everyday stress. This is part of the process of learning the language of the horse. When we learn his language this will unlock the door and release the barrier between us. When this door is opened we can explore all possibilities and expand our mutual understanding.

Breathe life into your training

An important part of this process is to discover the power we have within us which is enhanced by our breathing awareness. When we become more in tune with ourselves, the horse will mirror the smallest of changes. For instance when we release tension with a deep sigh the horse will release his stress allowing him to breathe more naturally. When we are riding, if we relax our facial muscles, mouth and jaw then the horse will feel this release and mirror our image. A relaxed jaw enables breath energy to flow down the spine. When the horse feels this comfortable release within the rider he will mirror this feeling. Yes, the horse truly does become our mirror.

When we make a deep outward breath from the core we release energy to direct the horse. The breath energy is directed towards the horse in both loose work and riding. The horse feels the energy release and moves away. Alternatively when we make a deep outward 'sigh' the 'energy' is not directed towards the horse. The release is just allowed to ripple down our body through to

The horse will mirror our heightened relaxed state of mind and body

our core and down into our feet. The horse does not feel any pressure from this energy but rather he will mirror our heightened relaxed state of mind and body.

Delfin – my greatest teacher

Many years ago I was introduced to Delfin at a famous stud near Seville in Spain. He was a highly energetic bullfighting stallion who was the most sensitive horse I had ridden. I then brought him back to the UK where we began to find ways to alter his highly charged nervous energy required for the bullring. I wanted Delfin to gain the confidence to relax within his work so that he could produce energy that enhanced his personality.

He has a huge character, which he has generously shared with students and clients as he willingly connects and leads them to a deeper understanding of the ways of the horse. Over several years now, he has become a true equine professor who has challenged me to re-evaluate many of my preconceived ideas on training and riding. He has opened many doors for exploration and I have been constantly challenged by the journey.

In the early days of riding Delfin, the boundaries of my knowledge were tested to the limit. We found consistency in our training very hard and an approach which seemingly worked on one day would yield a negative response when attempted on the next. I imagined that we had 'arrived' in our relationship after a few calm training sessions but then, for no obvious reason, I would be met with more resistance and anxiety. Delfin was capable on a good day of giving such a charmed artistic performance that people would remark they could sit and watch him all day, such was his great charisma.

During training on one particular day, Delfin refused to listen to my aids. My frustration grew, so my aids became stronger and stronger. His attention was on some mares galloping around a nearby field and he was just not willing to listen to his ineffective rider. After several minutes of the use of my legs and spurs having no affect whatsoever, I gave a deep sigh of despair. I then took a deeper inward then an outward breath and immediately I felt something different. Delfin was listening to me and responding. He moved forwards from my outward breath and as I inhaled he came to halt. I was amazed so I repeated the exercise with the same results. I decided to finish the session of training on this more harmonious note and wondered if Delfin would respond in a similar manner the next day.

I experienced huge anticipation before my next ride, but I tried to be calm and attentive to focus on my core breathing. Delfin responded immediately and I felt a huge feeling of elation as this highly sensitive intelligent horse was trying to teach me a huge lesson on how to match his sensitivity.

This experience led me to wonder if the techniques would only work with Delfin or whether other horses would understand.

I decided to explore further and I used similar aids through my core breathing with Maestu, my beautiful bay Spanish stallion. Maestu is a calm horse with a strong personality and quite the

> Delfin taught me a huge lesson on how to match his sensitivity

Maestu my beautiful bay stallion

opposite to Delfin in his nature. I was intrigued to find that Maestu was equally responsive and tuned in to these aids. Now Maestu has also become a teacher who has helped many people connect with a horse through the power of core breathing when riding.

For many years we have spent many hours discovering a deeper level of communication and Delfin inspires my students as he connects in a very spiritual way.

Recently we met a student who was very keen to learn more about the power of breathing and energy whilst training her horse. I demonstrated how she might use her body language to gain Delfin's focus and use the energy of herding to move him around the school. I then left her in the arena with Delfin to have some time to experiment with her core energy and body language. I was hoping to see Delfin connected with her yet moving away at walk, trot and canter. She would be the new lead mare of his herd. All I observed was a calm stillness between them. Delfin was standing facing her, totally connected mind to mind, yet with no instruction to move. Normally I would intervene and give further teaching, but for some reason I kept my distance and just observed them both. It was as if they were deep in conversation but I heard nothing. Their mutual focus was intense and I sensed an emotional exchange between them. I then asked Joanne, the student's close friend, if there had been a trauma in her life and I learnt that this girl, who was so in touch with Delfin, had suffered extreme abuse and trauma and wanted to make fundamental changes within her life.

Several weeks after this event I received a beautiful handmade card which included these words: 'I came to you looking for a new perspective on how I could improve my communication with horses, wanting to be the best person I can, for the horses in my life. I knew I was on an exciting journey but I didn't realise that I would find the real ME! My journey of self-discovery still has a way to go but my heart is now full with love and blessings for you both. The wisest teacher of all is the horse…'

Delfin had shown her that she did not need to be perfect or concerned that she was not good enough. She just needed to be 'herself' within the moment, to allow his spirit to make that

I want to be the best person I can for the horses in my life

The wisest teacher of all is the horse

connection. That was sufficient. That was all he asked of her. The horse has immense capacity to find a place for healing. He observes body language and is deeply connected with our feelings and emotions. Frequently we are not aware of the anger, sadness or fear which is buried deep within us. The horse wants to connect and make us aware of our true feelings and once we can express this inner fear, we create a place of peace and harmony where human and horse can experience *anam chara* love. The Celtic Christians use this expression to define a true spiritual love.

Delfin has created a place for healing for many people, where they understand more about themselves and gain the confidence to move on in their lives. I am frequently unaware of the hidden emotions of my students when they arrive, but Delfin often will tune in at a deep level and become a mirror of their mind. He instigates a release of emotion and does not fully connect until the student has acknowledged their own state of mind. In this way students learn from Delfin how to find the place mentally, physically and emotionally where the horse can connect and form a strong bond of trust. The horse can only place deep trust in a person who has self-belief and confidence, without false ego.

Delfin does not work with ego or false behaviour which again is very interesting to observe. He connects with the genuine reality and love of the individual and not the image they may prefer to portray. He seeks the true inner personality and not any false exterior. He responds to real love and joy from the heart.

> The horse responds to real love and joy from the heart

Making a connection

Over the years, I have ridden horses of different breeds and types and all seem to understand the language of breathing. I use core-breathing awareness from the time I walk into the stable to groom the horse. I try to keep my energy low and my breathing pattern deep and steady. I realise now that this is saying to the horse that he has a leader who will offer him calmness so he may relax and feel confident and secure within his environment.

Most people spend their lives talking, with more focus on the people and situation going on around them. Along with the amount of daily stress most of us carry as a weight on our shoulders, energy will become blocked if we disregard our physical condition and more harmonious core breathing. We almost disconnect from our physical awareness to become more deeply involved with cerebral energy. People communicate with an emphasis on verbal language rather than body language.

People communicate with an emphasis on verbal language

We are constantly processing information from what we can see and hear yet my feeling is that the horse seems more aware of our emotional state of mind and the signals of energy we give him. People may be more attentive to the spoken word but the horse is more perceptive to the mental, spiritual and physical state of a person and not convinced by the word that is spoken. The power of intention behind the word and the reassurance of a calm and confident leader will be the effective way to communicate with the mind of a horse.

We cannot disconnect our breathing from our emotions and most therapies will use breathing awareness to create a more relaxed state of mind. Yoga, reiki, aikido and tai chi all put great importance on methods of breathing to enhance both calmness and focus.

Many professionals now realise the importance of correct breathing practice whether they are actors, singers or serious sportsmen. A study of body relaxation supported by core breathing will connect us at a deeper level with our body, mind and spirit. Relaxation will help us to coordinate our movements so that we can allow fluidity to flow throughout our body.

Core breathing is an extremely potent tool because the power of less stimulation will very quickly create a more sensitive response. Our calm, focused state of mind will help us to communicate with more awareness and perception. The language of the horse is one of being constantly aware of changes in body language, tension and breathing, which would ensure his survival in his natural environment. One significant connection between man and horse is the deep outward sigh. You may have a horse feeling tense in his work; he could be an over-achiever always trying to please, or he may just be excitable and spooky, lacking in confidence. To restore a calmer attitude, just ride on a loose rein in walk or come to a halt. Then give a deep outward sigh to encourage the horse to release his tension. This form of relaxation can be repeated at regular intervals, throughout training and always at the end of a session of work.

Soon the horse will just take a deep sigh if he needs to release tension which will help to create a more harmonious relationship. This more harmonious approach to training will help to enhance good health and wellbeing for the horse.

If we teach the horse to move with deeper breathing patterns he will be able to move with more freedom through a relaxed

A deep sigh will release tension – allow it to happen often

ribcage and more fluidity throughout his body. We can learn to replace strong leg aids and spurs by using power and mobility within our core. This will allow the horse to breathe in a steady rhythm as constant pressure or nagging of the rider's legs against his ribcage will only destroy his natural movement.

Breathing and energy flow

Balance and energy flow can be controlled by breathing which will assist the horse in his own self-carriage.

Try this exercise; it demonstrates how core breathing can create more energy. Pick up a ball and throw it to a partner with no focus at all on your breathing. Before you throw the ball again, take a deep inward breath as you prepare to throw the ball. Then exhale strongly and direct the energy towards your hand as you release the ball. As you direct the energy from your breath into your arm, the ball will be thrown with much more intense power and speed.

Before you throw the ball take a deep inward breath to prepare for the throw

If we can influence energy through focus on our breathing when throwing a ball, how much more can we influence a sensitive horse?

Work under saddle

Once in the saddle, it is worth taking a few moments to check our **top-to-toe** posture as described in Chapter Three. Then make a very deep outward sigh, rippling down your upper torso into your core to release any tension. This will just relax your body, releasing tension through your muscles and joints. Allow the next inward breath just to happen in a natural way. Remember when you give a deep sigh it is just a gentle release of energy through your body. This is a different feel to the outward breath which directs the stronger energy from the core towards the horse and will instigate his movement.

BREATHE INTO WALK

When you feel calm and focused **top to toe**, take up an allowing contact with the reins, then inhale followed by a more vigorous outward breath. The exhalation will ripple down your spine releasing your core which encourages the horse to move forwards. This movement for the rider is similar to sitting on a swing and pushing it forwards and upwards, but it is much more subtle.

If your horse does not respond, use your legs once and, if needed, back up with a tap of the whip on your own leg. Very quickly the horse will tune in to this sequence of aids and respond from your breath alone. When the horse is walking forwards, continue breathing naturally and rhythmically with every stride. Imagine you are jogging and supporting your running with steady inhalation and exhalation.

Breathe into walk
....

BREATHE INTO HALT

When asking the horse to halt, your deeper inhalation will lengthen and strengthen your spine, creating stability and acting as a half-halt. As the horse responds, increase the inward breath, close your fingers on the reins and ask him to halt. Once the horse is standing still, release the pressure of your fingers on the reins, so that he can stand immobile in good self-carriage. Gain his focus with your steady core breathing. He should be calm and still, yet ready to move with your next deeper, energising exhalation. If the horse is allowed to stand, with only a light contact on the reins, his forward movement will be in lightness and not bearing down.

Breathe into halt
....

Transition from walk to trot

Prepare for the transition by walking forwards with a good energetic rhythm. Before you trot forwards ensure the horse is relaxed into a steady contact created from the propulsion of the hind limbs, enhanced by his attentive calm mind. Try to breathe steadily and naturally with awareness of expanding your core on the inward breath and releasing gently through your core on

Breathe steadily and naturally

exhalation. Take a deeper inward breath to prepare to trot. This will rebalance and further engage the movement, and gain his attention for a change in gait. Allow a deeper breath outwards and feel the energy ripple down through your spine, this will release the core and mobilise the seat. If the horse does not respond then use your legs, just once, and re-enforce with a tap of the whip if needed. Focus on regular natural breathing and use the deeper outward breath to instigate more energy. Tap once with your legs if the horse is not attentive to your energising breath. The horse will soon tune in to your breathing alone which will enable your legs just to hang in a relaxed way down either side of the horse's ribcage. In this way your natural balance will not be continually disrupted.

If your horse tries to pull and get too strong in your hand, rebalance with a focus on a deep inhalation and if necessary close your fingers on the reins. Your more intense inward breath will expand and strengthen your seat and core. This will give stability to the horse who will feel this momentary resistance to his forward movement. He will then rebalance and with a more allowing contact from your hand and fingers, you can encourage him to move forward with lightness. When you take the deeper inward breath, it not only lengthens and strengthens your spine but you will feel the tightness through your upper leg and thigh.

The horse is extremely sensitive to any change of balance or restriction from the rider. The feeling of restraint, which is a momentary check from the rider, will probably be sufficient to steady the horse.

The horse will quickly listen to core breathing as the first aid when asking for any change, whether in pace, gait or direction. Techniques of breathing will energise a lazy horse or, equally, calm an anxious horse. Breathing awareness will enhance communication between horse and rider; this will open up a path towards harmony and lightness. Whilst maintaining a focus on breathing, connect with the rhythm of the horse. Breathe naturally and rhythmically releasing the core to mobilise with the regular motion. You can even hum a tune, which helps you to connect both with your core and the rhythm of each stride.

Hum a tune to connect with your core

Breathing awareness will open up a path for harmony and lightness

You will begin to deepen your sense of connection, and picking up any tension or lack of energy flow within the movement will begin to come more easily to you.

TRANSITION FROM TROT TO CANTER

For this example, the transition is being made on the right rein. When preparing for the transition into canter, ensure the horse is well balanced in trot with sufficient energy and working correctly on the circle. Take a deeper inward breath and feel the horse rebalance, then take a longer and deeper exhalation whilst allowing your inside (right) shoulder and leg to move slightly forwards.

This slight shift in balance can be instigated from the centre of your core. Let us look at how you can make small, yet significant, changes in good balance, from your deep and centred core.

Whenever you make a slight change of balance or turn, think of instigating this from deep within your core. Place a hand about a couple of inches below your navel area and imagine deep within you there is a rope dangling in your centre (See *Centred awareness – riding a circle and changing direction* on page 123). Feel the slight turn of your whole body from this centred place. This allows changes within natural balance rather than moving only an arm or a leg which may disrupt your natural alignment.

Focus your deeper outward breath energy into the outside seat bone and allow a slight turn from your core to the outside (a small nudge to the left). Your inside shoulder and leg will move a little forward naturally and you will feel a release through your inside seat bone to accommodate the canter 'jump'.

As the horse learns to listen to your subtle aids and progress in his training, you will find that a simple deeper exhalation, directing energy towards your inside seat bone will influence the canter strike-off. At the same time allow your inside shoulder, seat and leg to come slightly forward. Instigate this movement from your centre which will allow the slight change of position to keep truly balanced.

The rider should be in balance and not tipped over to one side. The emphasis is on balance and weight distribution, using the power of the breath to release. To more fully understand this concept, practise standing in the **basic position** and become aware of directing your breathing into either your left or right side, down into your core. Breathe into your hands and your feet, and take time to explore the possibilities for energy, mobilisation and connection.

> Instigate any change of balance from your centre

VISUALISATION FOR CANTER

The upper body of the rider has to accommodate the space for the core to release for the uphill 'jump' into canter. Feel the elevation needed through your upper body to allow this movement. The upper body moves like a sail in the wind absorbing the motion of bounce. Sails capture energy, which influences the speed of the boat. Close your eyes momentarily to capture this feeling of flow and motion. Now, take a moment to imagine you are skiing. You speed down the mountainside absorbing the lumps and bumps of the snow through your ankle joints, knees and up into your core. When you are riding a horse, and engaging with his movement, it will be the core which absorbs and releases the movement. This will be the key to both stability and balance, the ability to 'go with the flow'.

The following exercise performed on the ground will help you to visualise this feeling. Walk for a few strides then prepare to take a step upwards, as if climbing a staircase. As you place your foot on the stair, your upper body has to lift to provide the space for your whole body to elevate.

This is similar to the more subtle feeling of elevation within the upper torso, when you ride. The power from the hind limbs of the horse will create more lightness and mobility in his shoulders. This elevation can become blocked if the movement is not absorbed by the upper torso of the rider.

Centred awareness – riding a circle and changing direction

You may find this concept described below an interesting technique to help to maintain the correct flexion, when you are riding on a circle. We looked at the importance of change in balance, being instigated from a centred core, during the trot to canter transition (see page 121).

Visualise a rope hanging heavily through your upper torso, down into the centre of your core, just below the navel area. This will be your true centre of gravity and balance. If you are aware of this strong centre, your movements will become more coordinated and less disruptive for the horse. Now picture a hand giving a small twist to the rope, just a couple of degrees. If you are on the left rein, this would be a small turn to the left. This will instigate a small movement from the centre of your core, which will be mirrored throughout your body. In this way you can turn in a natural, balanced frame. The horse will quickly mirror this slight change in balance. Your legs and shoulders will alter slightly in position, but the balance is instigated from your strong centred core, for the horse to follow. When you ride the circle on the right rein, the dangling rope in your core will be turned slightly to the right. This will naturally cause your inside shoulder to be brought backwards placing the outside of your body slightly forwards. In this way, the circle can be ridden in balance and lightness with minimal disruption for both rider and horse.

It is helpful to spend some time connecting with the horse, using only your seat. Walk the horse forward on a loose rein and feel how quickly he responds to the movement from your core. Just move forwards slowly and feel that deep, centred rope within your core give a small turn (or nudge) as you make a movement to turn to the left. Then walk forwards for several strides and repeat to the right. The horse will quickly mirror the changes from your core and balance. When you prepare for a change of direction, inhale deeply to rebalance, follow with an outward breath to release your lower back when you begin to change the rein. This focus will help to control the exercise.

Spend time connecting with the horse using only your seat, whilst walking forwards on a loose rein

Breathe into rein-back

When you ask the horse for rein-back, ensure he is standing four-square in good balance. If he has a hind leg resting or trailing behind his centre of gravity, take a deep breath in and then breathe out into the seat bone over the trailing hind leg. You can support the breath with a tap of your whip, if necessary, but your horse will soon listen to your seat bones if they become your initial aid.

Ask for the rein-back by closing the fingers on the reins and just take a deeper inward breath to prepare. When you exhale, direct the backward energy with your breathing, alternating from the left to right seat bone. Create a flow of backward energy from your core; imagine you are walking backwards. Allow your back and shoulders to absorb the backward and sideways motion. Once the horse tunes in to these aids, the pressure on the reins will become minimal as your core and change in balance will direct him.

Create a flow of backward energy from your core

Breathe into rein-back

Walking backwards yourself will be a helpful exercise for understanding this feeling. Place your hands on your hips and move back slowly, one step at a time. Feeling the backward rotation and swing of your hips will help you to mirror the movement of the horse when you are sitting in the saddle. Become aware of your spine and shoulders and the mobility you need to feel the backward and sideways motion. Then walk backwards with rigid shoulders and spine and feel how this tension restricts your backward movement. This will be mirrored by the horse if you are in the saddle and not allowing fluidity through your back.

Controlling the quarters

If you are riding on a circle and the horse swings his quarters out, direct your outward breath to flow down into your outside seat bone and leg. This will create a release and a flow of energy. The horse will feel this pressure and instinctively move away from the outside seat bone to become more centred under the rider. This technique of breathing into your seat bones can be used to improve feel and flow within all paces and gaits, lateral exercises and the more advanced collected movements.

The journey

Become both teacher and pupil

Every day will bring more challenges as we learn to become both teacher and pupil with our horse. Some days the more excitable horse will prefer to tune into the outward breath, which will suit his energetic mood and so we have to spend more time teaching him to connect with the deeper inward breath that can steady and calm him. The lazy horse may be more cooperative when responding to the inward breath as he will prefer to slow and rebalance using less energy. The rider will need to focus on energising the lazy horse by gaining a positive response to the outward breath aid. If the horse does not readily respond with more energy then support the breath aid by using the legs once giving a tap against his ribcage. If the horse ignores these aids, use the whip once, maybe against your own leg. The horse will soon learn that the outward breath will be quickly supported by stronger aids and will begin to respond to the breath alone.

Make sure that you have given the horse sufficient time to warm up and expend excess *joie de vivre*, either by working loose or on the lunge.

If we make a conscious effort to feel joyous when riding, our facial muscles will physically relax, which allows our spine to mobilise and flow with the movement. Our state of mind will control our physical ability to connect. These breathing techniques can be the essence of developing all ridden work through to advanced movements in collection. The essence of lightness and developing collection can become a feeling of just breathing with the movement.

These techniques are a journey of discovery which will reveal the depth of communication which can be built between horse and rider, breathing life into training.

Connect with creation

My deepest joy has been to observe the transformation as riders begin to feel more effective and connected with their horses through building awareness of their core breathing. When we feel connected mentally, physically and spiritually we are in touch with the universe and connecting with creation where our horse will feel 'at home' and secure. If we can teach the horse to work rhythmically whilst breathing more deeply, he can sustain more work whilst maintaining a healthy nourished body. Both human and horse come together in a moment of time. Humans so often feel disconnected not only with themselves but the environment around them.

Coordination is at the heart of true mastery and we need to feel truly relaxed with lower core energy to gain this control. It is fundamental to spend time reconnecting with nature through relaxation techniques and personal breath control.

Coordination
is at the heart of
true mastery

Chapter 5

Breathe Harmony into Collection

Heaven meets with earth when we
breathe the spirit of dance

— JENNY ROLFE

Dance for me my beauty, step out to the beat,

For even when there's silence I hear music in your feet.

So rhythmically you move, there's cadence in your stride,

As freely you move forward, your neck is arched with pride.

So balanced at all paces, with ease I read your mind,

For my reins could be of silk, your outlook is so kind.

So dance for me my beauty, show them we're as one,

Just as when alone in the early morning sun.

— MARY LASCELLES

Collection or restriction?

How would you define the word 'collection'? I looked this up in the dictionary and found words like 'gathering together' and 'pulling together'.

I then looked up the word 'together' and found such definitions as 'in sync', 'in concert' and 'as one'. These last words formed, in my mind, the picture of horse and rider performing classical art, in true collection.

When we understand what it means to 'collect' the horse, we can study in more depth the way to achieve this goal in our training.

Animals in the wild will breathe naturally, attuned to the environment and situation around them. They will respond to the laws of nature as they are at one with their world. When we ask the horse to become a part of our world he can find himself planted in a world totally foreign to him. We control him by placing a bit in his mouth, a bridle around his head, a saddle and tight girth around his middle and we may wear spurs and carry a whip. And sadly we don't stop there! The horse may then be subjected to reins, ropes and more gadgets tightening his neck and poll, creating pain and discomfort all in the name of schooling the horse. These accessories are meant to put the horse in a 'frame' but often the result is more akin to the restriction of imprisonment. Still we see the horse trying to please us and interpret our language. These methods may fail miserably as a dialogue of mutual benefit or empathy.

Let us take a look at the reality of the punishment we inflict on the horse when we ask for a 'fixed frame'.

Any athlete, whether human or equine, can only move freely when there is a lack of restriction to his head and neck, which need mobility to absorb all the movement. Visualise the power and energy as the horse jumps into the canter strike-off. The head and neck need to move forward to absorb this movement but if the rider has heavy hands the horse will only feel a restrictive tug in his mouth. In order to build the desire within the horse to step forwards with confidence, we need to build a relationship of trust, and the true foundation for this relationship is to ride with *more trust and fewer gadgets!*

The head and neck of the horse are not naturally placed over his centre of balance and so he will always need to compensate for any change in balance, which will be happening constantly in any movement. The head is positioned in front of the withers, which is the fulcrum. If the horse has too much weight unnaturally concentrated into a constrained head and neck, the whole spine will tighten. The whole centre of natural balance becomes disturbed. The tightness within the spine will not allow the hind limbs to support natural balance and carriage. The horse is also expected to carry the weight of the rider in this totally unnatural stance.

The true value of loose work is that when we can see the horse moving in graceful balance and posture with no tack at all, we can begin to understand that the connection we are looking

Ride with more trust and fewer gadgets

The horse moves with good balance and posture naturally

for is 'mind to mind' and 'breath to breath'. We have to learn to connect with the language of the horse and maintain the same language once in the saddle. We communicate through our core breathing, energy and balance.

So what is the impact on the horse when we try to control him with an array of gadgets and **only offer him our heavy hearts, strong hands and overloaded mind?**

Initially he will feel anguish which will immediately change his pattern of breathing. He may then take short and shallow breaths which will create future problems both mentally and physically.

Even when the rider is teaching the horse with enlightenment and empathy, certain tension will be created within the mind of the horse. This may not be from unyielding gadgets but merely from concentration during training. The horse will try hard to interpret our often confused signals and this can also have an impact on his pattern of breathing.

The philosophy of collection

Have you ever spent timeless moments looking over the gate of the field watching your horse when he is relaxing and grazing peacefully? Suddenly he sees something on the horizon which startles him and he gallops off with his head and neck in the air, full of fear and flight. Then he comes to a halt, understanding that he is not being threatened, but his initial excitement remains. Just as quickly the horse changes from fear to fun. His movement and balance now reflect his pride and poise and are reminiscent of those of the classical High School, executed with perfect grace and self-assurance. His neck is arched with pride as he displays both power and elevation, and he is displaying his natural talent for *true* collection.

When the horse moves in collection, his haunches begin to lower as they become more loaded with his body-weight. The hind limbs increase in flexion which gives more propulsion, and significant energy is created. This allows the horse more stability and increases his cadence. His spine and ribcage will natu-

> Take the time to observe the horse moving in graceful balance – with no restriction

The horse displays his natural talent for collection

rally elevate, enhancing mobility of his forehand and shoulders. When this process happens in a natural way the neck of the horse extends up and away from the withers demonstrating a 'proud' lengthened and arched neck.

During our training we are trying to emulate this pride within the horse to produce the gaits required for dressage. If we are aware of the nature of the horse, we can encourage his spirit to shine through. Our desire for 'perfection' and correct work can sometimes blind us to the individual character of the horse we are training.

To see a horse working with good impulsion and rhythm is to observe him moving with *joie de vivre* and energy, not with fear.

The biggest challenge for the trainer is not only to work towards gaining high marks within competition, but to form a good working partnership with a willing, athletic horse who is feeling both focused and confident.

Encourage the spirit of the horse to shine through

The physiology of collection

When we study the art of collection it is interesting to compare the similarities between ourselves and our horse. The power of core breathing is not only the foundation for good posture, balance and coordination for the rider, but has the same impact on the horse. Both human and horse can become better supported by strengthening core muscles and deeper core breathing.

> Core breathing – the foundation for posture, balance and coordination

When the horse learns to work with deeper rhythmic core breathing he can maintain better posture, which will help to maintain both the spine and the central nervous system. This system is responsible for coordination, balance and movement. When we sit on the back of the horse, an obvious and subtle connection is made between our core and his highly sensitive spine which houses his central nervous system.

Meridians, which are channels of energy, run through the body carrying electrical charges that move energy from one point to another. This is the subtlety of the central nervous system. Tension can create a blockage which restricts the natural flow. If we can communicate with the horse with respect and sensitivity, we can tap in to this subtle energy.

When we create strength and pressure with our legs against the horse's ribcage, this will tighten the motion of the ribcage as the horse naturally shrinks away from discomfort. This will have an impact on the freedom of movement within the whole body of the horse.

A human athlete will perform more effectively when wearing loose clothing as the fluidity of movement is not inhibited. He would be restricted if he was subjected to a bar in his mouth or gadgets pulling or pushing his body and asked to perform like a puppet. All athletes are working towards a fit and healthy body which allows energy to flow without restriction.

When the horse is tense his head and neck will be held high and tight which will impede the flow of movement through the spine. Injury and pain will be the consequence of a training programme that does not allow adequate time for the horse to learn to carry himself and his rider within a naturally balanced frame.

It takes time and patience to build a foundation of good muscles and ligaments to sustain the equine athlete as he progresses through his training.

When we place a tight leather band around the jaw of the horse, we restrict mobility through his head, poll, neck and spine. The relaxed horse should be able to chomp gently through a released jaw. A tight leather strap clamps the jaw together and of course, the mouth will be tightly shut. The art of training is to ride without these restrictions. If, therefore, the horse works with his mouth open, we can address the cause. It could be the stress of the moment or the rider's hands might be too heavy. Either way, if we are training horses we need to be aware of how he is feeling and not look for ways to mask his natural responses.

When I first rode Habil, my Lusitano stallion, he would noisily clench his teeth on the bit which was very unsettling. I used a French link snaffle bit and just a cavesson noseband, so if he was restless and unhappy with the bit in his mouth it was manifested for all to see. After many months together he now rarely shows this type of stress and if I feel his tension levels rising, I stop and sigh deeply, which he will immediately mirror. He then relaxes in his mind hence his jaw relaxes and we can continue with good energy and less anxiety.

> **W**hen the mind relaxes, the jaw relaxes

Tension causes restriction of movement and muscles will become tight which cannot physically support the natural flow of movement. Nature has given horses a helping hand with muscle development. When they are grazing with a low and natural neck carriage, the spine will be raised which enhances good effortless posture.

The influence of core breathing on the enhancement of performance

How can the influence of our breath have such a profound affect on our riding? A study of patterns of breathing has proved that core breathing can enhance relaxation and promote a sense of wellbeing and serenity. Once the mind has settled into the rhythm of the breath, you will begin to feel more connected, in body,

When grazing, the spine is raised naturally, which enhances effortless posture

mind and spirit. This is the essence of collection, to develop the bond and the feel of dance and empathy. You experience serenity as the mind begins to focus and becomes more empathic with the physical body. This creates a time for peace and reflection which induces feelings of warmth and tranquility.

As the energy of the dance is enhanced, your whole being can feel connection, moving as one with the horse and the pride of his nature. Our humanity finds a place with his nobility. When we understand how to feel peaceful and harmonious from within, we are in a good place for communication with the horse. The skills of training will be enhanced, if not transformed, by this awareness.

This is the path to true collection, in the same context of being, 'in sync', 'in concert' or 'at one'.

Core breathing will assist the horse in the following ways.

1. Prepare a calm and focused mind.

2. Help natural coordination and muscle development.

3. A precursor to good health and vitality.

4. Enhanced performance.

5. Support flexion.

6. Encourage good circulation to nourish all vital organs and muscles in the body.

7. Help to eliminate toxins from the body.

8. Allow movement to flow with fluidity, grace, balance and power.

9. **Core breathing** is a profound connection of empathy between human and horse.

Primary posture

Before we can develop collection we need to look at the primary posture in early training and also for warming up. This posture is long and low allowing the relaxed longitudinal stretch through a raised, mobilised spine. This allows a release in the neck and head to stretch downwards and forwards.

My philosophy for training begins with loose work in the school where I can get to know the horse as he works at liberty. I can quickly assess much about his nature and movement whilst also forming a connection with him, which provides a good beginning for our work and play together.

Young and untrained horses usually work with a natural balance that is more on the forehand. I have noted that when the horse is attentive and working energetically, he naturally releases through an elevated and fluid spine. He lowers and stretches his neck carriage by firstly taking it up and away from the withers and then forwards with a lowered head. If we allow him to do this, we can help the horse to work correctly and prepare him well for more collected work. He learns to move in a good, primary working posture which will be the key to developing collection in further training under saddle.

If we understand the nature of the horse within this unrestricted work, it will help us to determine the amount of energy and attention we need from each individual horse, to enhance

The horse learns to move in a good primary working posture

H elp the horse to control his balance without restriction

his natural talent. We can begin training the young horse to move, supporting himself with steady, deep core breathing. This is the first lesson to help the horse to control his balance without restriction.

Over time he will become physically stronger, with the ability to sustain his power, and a mind both focused and calm. Collection will evolve slowly through systematic exercises in training. Importantly, throughout the journey the spirit of the horse must be allowed to shine through as we cultivate a confident athlete who enjoys his work and relationship with his rider.

Taking up a contact

When training the young or immature horse we begin with the **primary working posture**. I prefer this expression to 'riding in a frame' as it encompasses the concept that we are working with nature and not wood! You can frame a picture or build a timber frame but when you ride a horse you are teaching a living creature, with a high energy force.

When you sit on the back of the horse imagine your centre of gravity and balance is deep within your core. If you pick up the reins and immediately replace your balance with more pressure through your arms and hands, this disturbs the whole centred feeling for both you and the horse. When riding, visualise your balance in the **basic position** on the ground and try to emulate the posture and stance whilst sitting in the saddle. Allow your arms to hang down either side of your body in a natural way with weighted elbows and lightness in your lower arms and wrists. As soon as you allow your elbows and wrists to become tight, you will be giving a backward force onto the horse's mouth.

If the horse is moving forwards well, without pulling, try to maintain a light, giving and elastic connection with his mouth. Focus within the moment so if you feel any change in energy, then the core breath can re-establish the connection you seek. You may need to reinforce core aids to be consistent so the horse will understand your leadership and power of intention. If the horse becomes tense then walk for a few moments and sigh deeply so that he learns to work with calmness.

Encourage the natural head carriage, not an artificially fixed carriage. Each stride will propel energy through the spine, which will slightly vary the natural position of the head. If the head and neck are forced into position by the hands of the rider, this will cause tension and discomfort. The horse should travel with his head just in front of the vertical or on the vertical and he may also bring his head in a little closer to his chest but this should be allowed and not forced. The head position is a reflection of the energy of the stride and his state of mind. Again, let the loose work become your teacher.

Correct training enhances the true beauty of the horse, both from the inside and out. As the horse progresses, so his posture will slowly cope with taking more weight through the haunches and hind limbs. The contact for the rider will become more refined and lighter as the forehand elevates naturally. A strong contact from the rider's hands will not allow the lightness and natural lift of the forehand.

I believe training using the primary working posture is good for the horse at every level of work. Even when you ride a more advanced horse, it will be beneficial to warm up in the primary working posture. During a training session when working a horse in more collection, this way of going will be helpful to relax the horse and encourage stretching through the top line, between the exercises.

The power of impulsion

Impulsion, within the context of training, describes contained energy – rather like a coiled spring. The power of the hind limbs creates a rounded loin and back which produces elevation and cadence within movement. The shoulders become lighter which is the path to developing collection through a correct system of training. The neck should not be compressed in any way and the head should be placed in a position of natural self-carriage – near to the vertical or slightly in front of the vertical – from a natural release of the poll area. This desired way of moving can only be instigated from a horse with a mind full of willing vitality, and yet producing calm and focused energy.

We are looking for energy but if the forward movement becomes too rushed or the strides too long, the horse will find it difficult to maintain his balance. Then the weight will be tipped onto the forehand, which will make it a struggle to maintain the equilibrium. It is fashionable to aim for bigger and longer strides but it is the balanced calm energy which produces the work to build a sound muscle structure for the athletic horse. Balance with energy is the key.

If we continuously ask for more energy, using strong legs, whip or spurs, then we need to review our methods of training so that less will become more.

The art of riding in lightness is to work with the mind of the horse so that although the work becomes more fun, there must also be discipline. If you are also in this frame of mind and enjoying your training, then he will be tuning in to your free spirit.

> Balance with energy is the key

Let us imagine a child at school attempting to learn a difficult, technical subject. The teacher who presents his knowledge with a blend of enthusiasm and imagination will be more likely to gain the willing concentration from a more relaxed and joyous student.

If we can influence the horse with a similar joy, his impulsion will become expressive as a result of his confident, enthusiastic mind, not as a result of rider domination, suppression or force.

When the horse begins to move, the natural initial motion comes from the head and neck. He must be *allowed* to move forward when we ask him to move. If we then restrict his neck and head, we are giving him conflicting aids which will become the enemy of elastic impulsion and true collection. Most problems encountered with neck carriage stem from a lack of propulsion from the hind limbs. How often have you seen riders pulling the head and neck of the horse into a tight contact and then kicking his ribs with legs and spurs? Again, the horse is receiving conflicting aids: the rider's hands are saying 'you cannot move

> Impulsion will gain expression as a result of a confident, enthusiastic mind

Horses have a great sense of play

forward' and the legs are instructing the horse to move away from the pressure. He has no place of comfort to go to and the tension begins to mount. Movement becomes stilted and the rider then blames the horse for not working forwards. Some training methods embrace extreme methods of contracting the head and neck of the horse, almost towards his chest. I don't believe that we should need to ask the experienced veterinary surgeon or physiotherapist if this is an acceptable way of riding. The expression of defeat and anguish in the horse's eyes, will give us the answer.

Riding towards balance and collection

Warming up

Self-carriage is gained through a system of warming-up exercises, which encourage the horse to produce a calm energy in his work. Our goals will be to achieve steady, submissive work from a highly active horse. The key to successful warming up will be to understand the nature and physical capability of your horse. Over a period of time you will find the routine that will best help your horse. For instance, I regularly use lateral exercises in a steady walk to create more suppleness and engagement. These exercises are an excellent preparation for balanced and more collected work.

In Chapter Three, we studied the importance of a sound **top-to-toe** preparation for the rider. It is equally important to prepare the horse with a thoughtful programme of exercises that will assist in developing his natural, athletic ability. To give this concept a more individual touch, we will look at some of the methods I use with my beautiful strong-minded bay Spanish stallion, Maestu.

Mentally and physically he is not naturally gifted to demonstrate the highest levels of collection. His conformation shows great power in the forehand and neck but his hind limbs and quarters are lighter and less powerful. He prefers to move with minimal effort and mobilisation of his joints. His true nature

Prepare with a personal top to toe

Use lateral exercises in a steady walk to enhance suppleness and engagement

complements this way of going as he is very steady and laid-back with the attitude that less is just enough! I not only need to enhance these qualities when we are training but also to instil him with some *joie de vivre*. We have, over the years, however, built a relationship and way of training where we can come together in energetic dance, connected by our core breathing. Here are some of the methods of training I use regularly to achieve this partner-ship with him.

WARMING UP FROM THE GROUND

Warming-up exercises will be as significant for the horse as the top-to-toe exercises are for the rider

Loose work has great value for warming up, and work on the lunge is beneficial for building the correct top-line muscles and encouraging work with impulsion. I begin by lungeing Maestu and when he has warmed up in all gaits, I trot him over two or three poles, about 6in (15cm) off the ground. This exercise really promotes active mobilisation of his joints and you can clearly see the stages as he progresses and begins to elevate through his spine. Initially his movement is minimal but after a few minutes he begins to show flexion through his joints which adds both cadence and elevation. This will be the key to advancing collection.

I lunge using the bridle, saddle (or roller) and side reins but I also sometimes just lunge from a head collar. When working over trotting poles I either use loosely fitted side reins or none at all. My aim is for the horse to be able to stretch naturally down and forwards through his top line.

Maestu being lunged over trotting poles

When Maestu initially comes into the school and is standing still, his hind limbs are often trailing out behind him. When he comes to halt after the exercises over the poles, his hind legs naturally come underneath him to better support his weight and balance. Because he is not a 'natural' the fruits of training are quite pronounced as our exercises help him to engage and collect in a positive way.

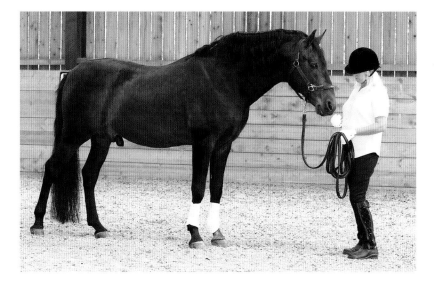

Maestu before work with his hind legs trailing out behind him

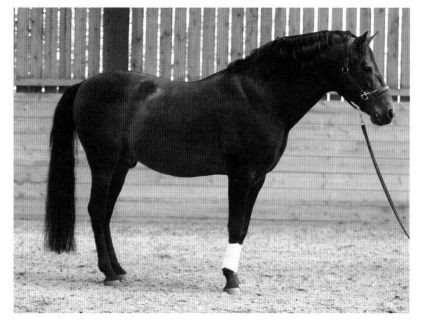

Maestu after work, stands with his hind limbs beneath him, supporting his body-weight and balance

I use a variety of different exercises over trotting poles. A particularly useful one is to trot in a circle and then halfway around, come down to walk. As he approaches the poles in walk I ask for an energetic trot about three or four strides away. He then trots over the poles with more elevation gained from the walk to trot transition. I try to keep him energetic whilst maintaining a steady rhythm. If he is allowed to rush forwards, the true value of the exercise is lost. I am looking for elevation and suspension with every stride.

Impulsion and energy are not only about the forward impulsion but the elevation and cadence, or time of balance off the ground, within each stride. This is the key to building self-carriage as the movement elevates to propel the horse forwards. There is more power and lift with each stride, which is on the path towards collection.

After a few minutes working on both reins we move to the next phase of warming up for Maestu, the exercises of the classical school, working in hand.

> Power and elevation with each stride is the path towards collection

In-hand work

INSTRUCTIONS FOR IN-HAND WORK

The art of working the horse in hand has been practiced for centuries within the classical school of riding. These well-established exercises are extremely valuable to enhance obedience and suppleness, with minimal confrontation. Work between the pillars is one of the original classical methods of training. When we are working the horse in hand, we replace the pillars, which would restrict the horse in his forward movement. We become moveable pillars and through our encouragement we can help him understand the movements we require. We will have a close contact with the horse when working from the ground, so we must ensure he respects our personal space. He must be encouraged to always work towards us and in close proximity with us, showing respect for our leadership and direction. He will learn to work with energy and with a greater understanding of the whip and voice aids. The touch of the whip will eventually be replaced by the seat and leg aids of the rider. The horse will gradually take more of his body-weight through his quarters and hind limbs which will be the foundation for developing collection.

A few minutes of lungeing prior to the work in hand will prove beneficial, giving the horse some time to warm up and work off any excess exuberance.

At first, just short sessions of work in hand will be sufficient. Aim to finish on a good note when the horse has responded well and understood his lesson.

We are looking for energetic 'bounce' in the strides, and so the horse must learn to move in lightness and self-carriage. The horse should work forwards energetically on the instruction of the handler. Equally, it is important for him to come back to halt with the whip placed quietly against his neck or croup.

IN-HAND EQUIPMENT

To commence work in hand, the horse should be tacked up as for work on the lunge with a cavesson, roller and lunge line. Side reins should be fitted, equal in length, allowing the horse his natural head and neck carriage. As with lungeing, we do not want to cause the horse to feel restricted but allow the top line of the neck to arch with the lower muscles relaxed. The horse's head should be aligned just in front of the vertical. As the horse will probably find the work easier on the left rein, it is good to begin in this direction.

The whip is used to reinforce communication with the horse and certainly not as a form of punishment. It may tell him to 'work forwards', 'more energy' or 'whoa' but should never be used in frustration or anger.

The whip may be used to communicate in three different ways whilst working the horse in hand.

1. To encourage forward movement. A light touch or tap will say, 'walk over' or 'walk on'.

2. To ask for halt. The whip can be placed gently against the neck/ shoulder, or anywhere on the body This action together with a gentle voice command will be the signal for halt. The whip should remain lying gently against the horse until he responds and, once he has come to a halt, the whip pressure should be taken off, away from his body. This command will be taken over by the rider's legs in the ridden work. The rider will place his legs well on the girth to halt, then relax the pressure immediately the horse responds.

3. To create energy in movement. In more advanced work the whip may be used with quick, light 'electric' touches to produce more activity for such movements as piaffe and passage.

FIRST IN-HAND EXERCISE: WALK AND HALT

Position the horse on the long side of the school and prepare to walk on the left rein (anti-clockwise). Calmly stand facing the horse with the line from the cavesson in the left hand and the whip in the other. The horse is then encouraged to walk towards you, so be prepared to take a step backwards if necessary to allow the horse enough room to move in your direction. Stand in front of the horse, with a relaxed body posture. With your voice and small vibrations with the lunge line, encourage the horse to take a few steps forward. Walk backwards, very slowly and after a few strides ask for halt. Do this by taking a deep in breath to increase your body stature and create a 'wall of restriction' with your body energy. Use your voice calmly, placing the whip gently on the neck to halt. When the horse responds, praise him with your voice and a gentle stroke of his neck. It is important that the horse should always works towards his handler, to promote a forward-thinking horse when working in hand. Repeat this exercise, encouraging the horse to walk forwards and come back to halt.

> Promote a forward-thinking horse

When the halt is established it is important to take the whip quietly away and lower it gently. For the horse, the quiet instruction and aids will always become his reward for obedience. The horse should remain calmly in halt until given further instructions.

These new ways of training may cause the horse some tension and so it is important to use communication with voice, body language and breathing awareness to help the horse to relax.

INTRODUCING WORK ON THE SMALL CIRCLE

The introduction of these exercises on the small circle will help to improve both control of the shoulders and activity of the hind limbs.

Exercise on the small circle – left

Prepare to circle left and position yourselves in front of the horse, turned slightly to face him from the right-hand side. You will need to be in a position to look into his eye and, with eye contact and body position, be prepared to block his forward path. Initially, it is preferable to have a helper until the horse is familiar with the exercises. The extra handler can encourage the hind legs to mobilise around on the circle. The horse's head should not become tilted but remain in the vertical position. The flexion of the neck will be away from the direction of the movement, as in leg-yielding.

To circle anti-clockwise, hold the lunge line with the left hand, with the horse's head and neck on your left. Holding the whip in the right hand, encourage the horse, with voice, body language and whip, to commence walking a circle around you. He should be moving his inside limbs laterally to cross in front of the outside limbs. The front legs should cross over as if performing a turn on the forehand. After a few strides ask for a halt and then repeat the exercise for just a few strides.

Be prepared to move a step or two backwards, as the horse circles around you. He must have sufficient space to mobilise his shoulders, to step **forwards** then across. If he is given too little room for movement, he may take a backward step which is totally incorrect.

When this exercise is carried out correctly the horse will demonstrate greater elasticity of movement and his strides will promote more elevation and self-carriage. These movements should be carried out with **steady precision** to maximise the potential for true cadence.

This small-circle exercise should be executed near the long side of the school. Whilst on the circle, as you reach the outside track again, the horse can be taken up the long side in shoulder-in for a few strides before repeating the small-circle exercise, which is akin to a turn on the forehand around a small circle.

This is intense work for the horse, so do the exercise for only a few minutes initially. Reward every effort made by the horse and keep the pace steady and calm at all times as tight muscles will restrict mobility and may cause damage if the horse becomes very tense. This type of work can also be performed without tack; I have seen the greatest results by incorporating loose work at all levels of training. The loose horse soon learns to perform these movements from both body language and breathing techniques. This type of liberty work will enhance the communication skills between both horse and rider thus developing the **art of communication**, a friendship-building trust and harmony, which will be taken through to the ridden work. Once completed on the left rein, repeat the exercise on the right rein.

Reward every effort made by the horse

Maestu working on a small circle, in hand on the right rein (above), and at liberty on the left rein (left)

Search to reach the soul of the beautiful horse

Below is a study written by Christine who brought her beautiful Spanish stallion to me. Christine has spent her life with horses and from an early age she was busy gaining her BHS qualifications. She had the opportunity of learning classical principles with Baron Blixen Finecke and then began producing show horses which were taken to County level.

When I asked Christine, what she really wished to achieve from her time with me, she responded with the words, 'I want to reach the "soul" of my beautiful Spanish stallion.'

Christine's study describes the possibilities for exploration when we focus on core breathing and become aware of our own body mastery and energy. Christine began by mastering the core breathing techniques, then took her stallion through specific in-hand exercises to improve his collection.

Case Study CHRISTINE AND DANILON, SPANISH STALLION

My relationship with Danni was not developing as I had hoped when I sought out Jenny for her foundation body-breath awareness and control course. Danni was tense, holding his ribs out stiffly, and I was tense, unable to move him forward enough to engage his hindquarters from my aids. As a stallion he performed obediently just what was requested but didn't show any joy in the school exercises. Danni regarded our time in the school as 'brain food' and his duty, with an occasional explosion of excess energy. Perhaps you may feel that I am being overly anthropomorphic in my relationship with the horse. As a rider the time that I spend with my horse is a personal and

magical time, always to be polished and honed for the time that fate awards us together. So I approached Jenny to see how we could develop further or as I put it to 'find Danni's soul'

The core-breathing exercises were revelations to me, as the air – the stuff of life itself – released and straightened my body, softly lifting my upper body and then coursing down to gently move my pelvis forward as I exhaled using my core correctly. After the first day, I was curiously aware of this new sensation – feeling like 'a bee with a tail' as I returned to my bed and breakfast that night! Danni, during his day training, had joined up with Jenny when working loose in the school; sharply

→

pricking his ears as he made his decision to let her be part of his life as he followed her around.

And so we started a new journey together finding a softer, more personal communication with Jenny's words 'light, light, light' following us as we worked through the transitions using the rhythm of the breath to allow and release the pelvis, as appropriate, to influence the movements. As you sit in a chair while you read this, take a breath in and feel how your weight will shift over your seat bones, and then softly breathe out and observe the travel and release of your body-weight on said seat bones to mimic the sensation.

Jenny addressed other issues in my personal body language, which was not assertive enough for a stallion. It gave Danni mixed messages of what I wanted from him and so, of course, stopped a vibrant, considered communication. Possibly the hardest exercise for me was finding my personal energy. All of my life I had learnt to sit quietly and find an inner stillness on fairly gassy horses but now I had to learn to project my energy forwards for my laid-back *Pura Raza Español* stallion to encourage him and find that personal link that is part of movement. Most people know someone with a 'hot seat', well I have the opposite, sending most horses straight off to sleep!

Our final session together was the approach to collection, working to show

Danni how to step forward towards the hand, from the lightest possible aids. Jenny repeated to me several times to lengthen the reins again until Danni was ready, and then, as he found his true balance and rhythm, I felt a lightness and softness to the swing of his back that I had never felt from him before and with it came contentment. Danni was happy at last.

Jenny's techniques have been incorporated into my everyday life. For example, just walking along the lane to collect the brood mares, I practise using the breath to release and free the pelvis and when handling the young horses I utilise the body language that Jenny taught me. I centre my life force to the ground with my breath and breathe in to ask them to halt. Even the youngest foal immediately and effortlessly understands what is needed. The gangling youngsters manage to balance themselves and stay in a place to comply with the daily routine of simple handling.

For Danni, Jenny suggested a series of in-hand exercises as we had limited space to work at home. We started with a simple yielding of the hindquarters to loosen and mobilise the hind leg development.

As we worked each day his head, neck and general carriage gradually lifted creating a shorter more collected outline and, as my husband pointed out, the more erect and poised my carriage the better Danni performed the exercises. I felt less pressure (self-created) to succeed working

→

Danni working in hand

in this way and felt a greater awareness of the harmony of each movement and a more holistic understanding of the process of engagement of the quarters.

As the weeks turned to months I noticed that my legs could now drop easily over Danni's ribcage finding their natural position as he relaxed and breathed more easily and he would sigh contentedly as we reached home or as we paused to let heavy traffic disperse. When I felt tense, if say horses were galloping in a field beside the road as we hacked past, I would remind myself to follow the core breathing pattern to control my tension. This would help my balanced position and Danni would respond by staying calm and focused on me. He would sometimes respond with a deeper outward sigh to reassure me!

As we worked into the summer, I felt his balance improve and increase, allowing his self-carriage to improve until, at last, I felt his energy was held under my seat; the start of a new symmetry of movement and the fruition of a new relationship.

Collection for the rider

The horse mirrors the rider and so if we are to be successful at riding in lightness, balance and collection we need to understand the posture of collection for ourselves. We cannot expect to suddenly jump into the saddle and be instantly balanced in body, mind and spirit unless we take some time to build more discipline and awareness in our everyday lives. We have looked in detail at various exercises to gain self-awareness and balance, which are fundamental to becoming an effective rider. The time spent in preparation from the ground is of paramount importance.

It is useful to practise walking around the school, visualising the **top-to-toe** posture described in Chapter Three. Begin to feel really tuned in to your core breathing and become aware of your posture. Now raise both your arms and hands, stretching upwards, high above your head. Keep your energy deep and low in your core but feel the elevation and expansion within your ribcage and feel the power of your breathing both wide and full. Soften your eyes and sense the energy flow of the breath creating both space and lightness in your upper body. Then gently lower your arms and continue walking slowly. Do you feel lighter and more buoyant through your upper torso? This is the feeling a rider should establish when developing collection. When we are totally self-aware, we gain control and influence. For instance, the horse may have good energy but his rhythm may be too fast. If we steady our pattern of breathing and slow the rhythm of our seat, the horse will mirror our balance and begin to use his energy with more calm elevation in his gaits. The breath can be used to strengthen our core or, by using more gentle breathing, we can relax through the core.

There are as many ways to breathe as waves in the sea and so explore and listen to the horse as he responds to your subtle energy. You will become less aware of distractions and disturbances as you build on your connection.

Explore and listen to your horse as he responds to your subtle energy

Balance and symmetry

True balance comes from symmetry of both horse and rider

True balance comes from symmetry of both horse and rider

When you ride forwards on the straight line, try to ensure that you have straightness. In other words, feel that the horse is balanced, not leaning and feeling more weighted to one side. He should be working purposefully forward, feeling centred underneath you, with both hind limbs tracking up with equal energy to propel the horse forward in balance. You cannot ask for true collection if he is moving through a spine which is crooked and not well aligned. Balance comes from symmetry of both horse and rider.

I was building a training programme for my stallion Habil and I decided that I needed to spend time working on his basic gaits moving forwards and straight. Habil had been trained to look spectacular in his movements, but he was working with too much anxiety, hence the natural looseness and straightness within his gaits had been neglected.

I also found problems on the right rein, where he tried to fall out through the left shoulder. I went back to the valuable lateral exercises in steady walk, working primarily in shoulder-in, pirouettes, turns on the forehand and leg-yielding. I would just ride a few strides of one exercise then change the rein to ride and rebalance through further exercises. When he felt more equally balanced I asked for a transition into trot. Habil would then move with more equal activity in his hind limbs and also there was more release through his whole body. The lateral work had improved his fluidity and enhanced his symmetry.

When we study technique in horsemanship we find that, on its own, this is not enough but if we expand our knowledge of theory to include control and coordination in mind and body we can take technique to a more profound level. If the rider is sufficiently aware of letting go of tension he can then connect with his natural centre and inner being. As long as we live and breathe, we will always convey a message to the horse, whether it is anxiety and anger or joy and security. Our energy and body language will give positive signs of relaxation owr manifest our higher levels of stress. Without discipline and focus, our thoughts within the moment are few and far between. It is the essence of communication to cultivate awareness and authority so that we understand the impact we have on a horse. There can be no true collection without mutual empathic connection between horse and rider.

> Technique in horsemanship is not enough

Visualisation: paint a picture of collection

True impulsion comes from the heart. The horse who can perform with vitality and pride will be feeling confident with his rider, seeking to please his leader. Impulsion is not only a visual and technical goal for the trainer, but a way to stimulate pleasure and cooperation between horse and rider.

Paint a picture in your mind of the relaxed rider with a lengthened relaxed neck, released jaw and mobility of the shoulders. The rider is aware of deeper core breathing, which will enhance

> True impulsion comes from the heart

Breathe into allowing shoulders

lower back stability. More emphasis on controlled, steady core breathing will support the upper torso as it absorbs the extra elevation of collection. Breathing into allowing shoulders supports the movement of the spine. This enhances fluidity as energy is harnessed and released, like a wave in the sea.

The core becomes stronger but maintains mobility and the upper torso lengthens and strengthens with this pattern of breathing. It encourages a feeling of pride and lightness in the upper body which can efficiently absorb the elevation of the horse within collected balance. We talk about core stability for the rider but this is also an important goal within training for the horse.

Paint a picture of collection in your mind

Now paint a picture in your mind of the horse with a lengthened relaxed neck, a released jaw and mobilised shoulders as a result of calm yet energised movement and deep regular breathing.

The rider with core stability and mobility can melt and flow whilst gaining the feel of lightness and energy through the upper body. Rhythmic core breathing will help the chest to elevate and expand as the rider uses the breath to enhance self-carriage. This expansion creates more buoyancy so that the horse can carry the balanced rider in more lightness. The rider sustains steady contraction and release through the spine and relaxes the jaw which, when pushed back gently, enables the head to be supported in balance. When the head is supported through lengthening the back of the neck, the whole body energy can flow from head to toe as the spine becomes re-aligned. Every stride towards collection is ridden with an uphill feeling which can be assisted by a depth of feeling of pride and joy from within. The power of the breath will enhance this wave of mobility so that the rider can feel at one with the horse. The rider who is aware of sitting in good posture and lightness becomes a picture of *human* collection and self-carriage. Again, use techniques of visualisation to paint this picture in your mind.

These breathing techniques are the essence of developing further lightness, cadence, collection and moving on into passage, the ultimate 'dance' for both horse and rider.

Chapter 6

My Journey with Habil

> The horse is a reflection of the truth
> from your heart
>
> — JENNY ROLFE

Open your heart and eyes

Have you ever been in a close relationship or experienced long-term friendships that span the years? If so, how would you respond if you were asked to write down a formula for success within a relationship? I would imagine the qualities of trust and caring along with empathy in communication and the ability to listen would be extremely important. The ability to lighten up and have fun could also be high on the list. Spending quality time together would be significant, to nurture the growth of friendship. Nothing in life stands still. We should grow, expand and explore or we could be on the path to becoming fixed and static. All creation is meant to evolve.

Let us now think about what could create the breakdown or destruction of a close friendship. For instance, if your dearest friend hurt you, by breaking your trust and confidence, would you be quick to forgive and forget or would you start to question their integrity as a friend? Abuse of trust and confidence is often the precursor to a breakdown of affection and love.

And what does the word 'love' mean to you? The Celtic Christians used the words *anam chara* to describe a 'soul friendship'. I make no apology for coming back to this description which was included in the introduction of my book, *Ride From the Heart*. I have gone full circle but is this not the essence of life?

Anam chara

Soul friendship — a relationship built on trust

Anam chara love is used to describe a relationship built on trust, where communications are 'face to face', a reflection of truth from the heart.

Anam chara love describes the ability to become a mentor and express leadership.

Anam chara friendship demands humility yet honesty and displays the art of listening based on a desire to acquire knowledge.

Anam chara friendship searches for a quiet place of truth.

This is the relationship that I seek with the horse, as there can be no progress in training without humble, honest and wise leadership. We talk much about technical goals but without these qualities, schooling and training have little value.

If we can incorporate *anam chara* friendship, we will gain respect and trust from the horse. The gifts for us will be profound and we too will gain greater self-respect and inner peace as we grow to believe in these concepts and philosophies. The horse will become our reflection, the mirror of our mind.

> *Anam chara* – soul friendship – reflects the truth from the heart

Habil my *anam chara* friend

Recently a profound teacher has come into my life. I have spent years learning and teaching the wisdom that had been revealed to me by horses, but Habil has become an amazing influence upon me. His extremely perceptive and sensitive nature has made me dig deeper to explore new territory of connection and communication.

We have looked at the importance of building trust within a relationship and this has been the key, along with consistent patience, to building an incredible bond with Habil; a true *anam chara* relationship.

We can share joyous moments when we are on the same wavelength, yawning or laughing, working or just being together. Under saddle he responds to every nuance of my core breathing and any change or inflection of physical tension. I know if I breathe with more uphill core energy, he will immediately dance into passage and if I change to breathing with more forward energy he will respond with forward impulsion. He has truly become the mirror of my mind. This brings with it the need for greater discipline and responsibility for my own self-awareness.

Habil came to me as a very respectful, educated stallion who was stabled for much of his life and brought out to 'do a job'. He was very anxious and my first thought was to change his state of mind and help him to enjoy a more relaxed attitude in the school.

Habil's anxiety would build as soon as he saw me taking the saddle into the stable, even before I placed it on his back. This could simply have been his sensitive nature reacting to the thought of having the girth tightened (which I do very slowly) but his reaction to the bridle told me another story: he would swing his head away and make it very difficult for me to put the bridle on.

I used my lowered body demeanour and relaxed head and shoulders to encourage him to lower his energy. I also put some honey on the bit to try to make this a more positive experience for him but this was not such a good idea as we ended up get-

We share joyous moments together

ting rather messy! It did, however, begin to help him release and relax so that he was chomping the bit rather than grinding it with his teeth. Until he lowered his head to receive the bit, I did not attempt to put it in his mouth. If you have to reach up to a horse who is pulling away from you, the battle has commenced. I refuse to do this, which means being prepared to wait. Patience does pay off though in these cases, as it did with Habil; he soon became more accepting and relaxed about having the bridle put on.

When we first started working together, the moment I was in the saddle, he would grab the bit and grind it noisily between his teeth. I rode with a light contact as I was convinced the only way he would settle down was to feel more relaxed about being ridden in the school. I did check his teeth for any problems but found nothing to cause this response. This was a horse who had performed with too much anxiety and little pleasure. Over the course of many months, I sought to allay his fears. In the early days, as always, I introduced the loose work which really helped me to assess the changes in his personality. The first time he was taken in the school, for loose work, he just stood there, looking around him. He did not move or know what to do with himself. I then cracked the whip and encouraged him to move around. After a few seconds, he exploded violently, galloping and bucking around the school, but still looking very anxious. After a while he calmed and I began to use more body language to direct his path. I blocked him and he turned and we repeated this routine, two or three times. Then I used my body language to instigate a circle and he began to circle around me. I focused on my calm energy and breathing. I took the decision not to ride for a while but to give Habil time to settle down in a new country with a different routine and environment. He had never experienced liberty whether in a field or school so I spent time letting him graze for a short spell each day. I could not leave him too long as he was anxious and almost seemed to gain security within the confines of his stable, partly perhaps because there is a great bond between the stallions as they all enjoy being in close proximity to each other.

Each day I took Habil in the school to work him at liberty as this gave him time to utilise his energy and begin to form a

Allow a horse to be a horse

bond of trust with me. I realised he was still very agitated in the school and so I decided to show him that he had permission to roll. He was far too stressed to do this naturally, without a leader to instruct him. I lowered my body stance and pawed with my leg and quite soon he mirrored my actions. It was wonderful to see him relax and allow himself some time just to be a horse. It took no time at all before Habil decided the school was for fun and rolling, which for a while I did my best to encourage. When his attitude became more relaxed in the school, I just changed the sequence. I stopped giving him the initial time for rolling and play and began to introduce the lungeing and ridden work at the beginning of the session; then, after the ridden work, I would take off his tack and allow the loose work and play, in order to observe his state of relaxation and connection.

This was the beginning of our journey to inspire his confidence and work with his new found trust and friendship.

Over time our relationship developed through the loose work and he would connect with me on the circle, even performing a passage when I attempted to perform one myself! My elevated knee action and purposeful, more powerful core breathing seemed to connect with his mind and he joyously rose to the occasion. When we first started the loose work Habil would canter off down the school to see himself in the mirror but as our bond increased he began to focus on me more and more. This relationship has grown and now after the loose work has finished he will walk over and follow me wherever I go. This has its comical side because, when I am doing a demonstration with the stallions, Habil insists on standing with me when I am teaching and follows me like a shadow, even mirroring my emotions: laughing or sighing. I think he has become quite a comedian!

I once experimented by lying down in the school. I had gained sufficient confidence in our relationship to know he would not harm me if I was sitting or lying down on the ground.

Habil walked over to me and just stood over me with a lowered neck and head. It was akin to a mare guarding her foal. He did not move until I began to get up and walk away, when he continued to follow me in every direction I chose to go.

Habil will
follow me
wherever
I go

Use your instinct and intuition when working with horses and you will rarely be misinformed!

If I run across the school Habil will canter after me, with no attempt to come into my space or threaten me, but just to be with me.

I now use loose work as part of our normal training regime as, even after I have ridden Habil, I take off his tack in the school. I can then connect through the loose work to ensure our bond is true. If for instance I had been a little too demanding in the ridden work, he would walk off and disconnect from me within my large school. I do not work in a round pen but in a large indoor school where the opportunist horse may easily evade instruction.

Most of the time, when I take off his tack he stands and waits for instruction then works around me in a circle, looking joyous and free in his spirit. He is the servant no longer, but an empathic friend and teacher.

The loose work reveals the truth. If you are harsh and unforgiving in the ridden work, your horse will not want to connect with you at liberty. The horse will become your teacher and you his pupil.

Loose work reveals the truth: the horse will become the teacher, and you the pupil

Lessons from Habil

I spent many weeks working in the school with Habil at liberty before I felt the time was right to re-introduce training under saddle.

Let me paint a picture for you of Habil under saddle before I began training him. He constantly gripped the bit in his mouth crashing it against his teeth, which was very distracting. He was very athletic in all his movements but had become used to working through a compressed spine and had become rather abrupt and staccato in his rhythm and movement. His neck was arched but compressed because he had been ridden in a double bridle by a rider with rather strong arms and hands. Habil's energy was highly charged and extremely reactive and on a scale of one to ten for instant reaction, he would have scored nine or ten. This was not only in the school but also when being handled generally. When ridden, I felt his energy was rather like sailing in a turbulent sea, full of excess, erratic energy and changes in balance.

The picture of Habil I was trying to create was a horse more relaxed, yet attentive, with the ability to move forwards and stretch down through his neck to mobilise his back. His head, neck and jaw would be much more relaxed, just chomping gently, accepting the bit in his mouth. The canter work would feel softer, more comfortable and not so stilted, with more flowing harmonious movement. I wanted to see him release his own tension naturally by taking a deep sigh and training with joy and less apprehension. Habil needed to feel sufficiently calm to stand still, comfortable in his own skin, to be more peaceful and yet responsive. I would look for the gradual changes in muscle structure as I groomed him, noticing more supple skin and a more developed top line within a relaxed, natural posture.

Visualisation for Habil

In the early days with Habil, I would sit in the saddle and feel his tightness and anxiety. He was so quick to respond and I wanted to find a way to steady his mind. I had to think carefully about my

Picture flowing and harmonious movement

Paint a picture of the horse in your mind and then ride that picture thoughts and feelings. It is a natural response when sitting on a tense horse to mirror his state of mind, so the discipline of **top-to-toe** posture awareness (see page 92) becomes really significant as a positive aid for connection and calmness. I also used the power of visualisation and imagined it was a warm and sunny spring day, even though the wind was howling outside on a bitter, cold morning. I pictured the serenity of sunshine, flowers, trees and a sense of calmness.

Visualise riding on a warm spring day through a field of flowers

As I visualised these thoughts, I embraced the warmth and tranquility and, both physically and mentally, I felt lighter and more relaxed. I felt my jaw release into a smile which allowed my body energy to flow freely. The ride became more joyful and Habil began to mirror my happiness. This created further release and energy flow down my spine. I imagined flowing into transitions with the lightness of a small wave, lapping against the sand. I normally visualise energetic upward transitions, but Habil already had so much energy, my thoughts needed to try to regulate his responses.

Each of our emotions engages a physical response

This endorses the principle that our mind controls our body. When we learn to use techniques of relaxation and visualisation to control our mind and thoughts, we can then, and only then, gain control of our body.

I reiterate: each emotion and thought engages a physical response. If we are relaxed we release tension, if we are angry we become physically distressed. To become influential riders we can use the power of core breathing and visualisation to help us.

Training with Habil

Habil has a charm about him as he always wants me to think that he is simply the best, a real superstar. Underneath this compliant attitude is a horse who can suddenly become quite dominant and who would love to give me *his* instructions if I allowed it. His mood can change as quickly as the next breath and I have to be extremely perceptive. He can be quite a challenge to ride if you are looking to maintain steady energy. When I sit in the saddle, I feel his eagerness to get going. The balance can so easily change: one moment I am leading the dance and then in a very subtle way he tries to rearrange the dance and take the lead. I am sure you have experienced that feeling!

Lead the dance

Detailed below is the warm-up session I used in the early days of training with Habil and some of my methods used to calm him and gain more empathy with his responses. As time has gone by he has become much more attentive and calm in his attitude. He is now more consistent in his responses and harmonious within his gaits. You may find the methods I talk about here helpful to you if you are experiencing problems with a horse showing excess anxiety and stress in his work.

I tried to build on Habil's positive, joyous energy to create self-carriage and work towards collection, in the true spirit of dance.

THE WARM-UP

I would begin with loose work to assess Habil's mood and build on our connection for the day. After a minute or so of Habil trying to look at himself in the mirror, he would then begin to give me his full attention. It took a few minutes for him to really tune into my presence, breathing and body language.

Once in the saddle I focused on a connection with my core whilst riding forward with a very loose rein contact. His walk was free and forward and I could sense his keenness to get going! I felt that he was not really tuning in and listening but rather walking off more independently. I responded with a deep inward breath which gave me strength and stability. Sometimes Habil would come to halt, which was too great a response, as I was looking for a steadier stride but the fact that he had begun to listen made me feel pleased. I then released an outward breath and felt my core energy directing him to move forward again. If he bounced off into trot, I knew that I was over-breathing and that less was going to be more on that day!

I reflected on my **top-to-toe** system and assessed my body awareness (*see* overleaf). Giving a deep outward sigh, I released some tension, and tried to achieve a feeling of light energy.

I had to ensure that I focused on straightness as Habil was rather like a wriggling worm and easily placed his quarters inwards or outwards. I discovered that as we built on impulsion, his hind action gained momentum and he became more aligned and straight in his body and movement.

True collection can only be achieved through straightness of the spine as unequal loading of the quarters can cause harm to joints, muscles and ligaments.

True collection is achieved through straightness

Reflecting on my top-to-toe basic position

Seek a centred feeling from deep within

I would then begin to ride some changes of direction in the school using, for example, diagonal lines and serpentines. My initial aid came from my core so that Habil felt my change of balance from our mutual centre. On the left rein I kept a light rein contact and asked Habil to begin circling across the school from my core but he wouldn't listen and wavered to the right. I then took up a little more connection with the reins, still light but with more contact. I checked my weight distribution and directed my outward breath down to the outside seat bone, thus allowing more weight down into my outside seat bone to support my outside leg aids to correct any wavering to the outside. I made small adjustments from the centre of my core. It was not a focus on turning shoulders or peripherals but a centred feeling from deep within.

Once the circle continued with correct flexion and energy, we could then execute some serpentine loops to continue to supple and gain his compliance. I then asked for canter on the left rein, being aware of my out breath flowing down through my inside seat bone. I slightly twisted the rope deep in my core centre towards the right, which brought my left side slightly forward and released my left shoulder and seat bone to relax into the canter jump.

This action also allowed an upward and outward energy flow from my stomach up towards my hands. I encouraged Habil to canter forwards with good impulsion and lightened my seat so that he could mobilise through his back. I played with the variations in canter and used more energetic breathing to encourage forward impulsion. After the first phase of warming up we walked on a loose rein and prepared for the lateral exercises in walk.

LATERAL EXERCISES IN WALK

I used lateral exercises in walk from my earliest training sessions with Habil and, in fact, use these exercises with most horses to gain suppleness, engagement and also a calm attentive mind. Steady and precise exercises in walk hold the key to gaining a more supple and balanced athlete who is capable of working in a good natural self-carriage.

With Habil I focused on building a connection through engagement of his hind limbs. I rode the steady lateral exercises of shoulder-in and half-pass in walk, and then straightened and changed direction to ride shoulder-in and pirouette. One exercise flows into another, akin to moving around a dance floor, whilst remaining in walk. I also performed under saddle the small-circle exercises used when working in hand. These exercises are precise and steady, allowing muscles to stretch and flow.

> Lateral movements have a natural ebb and flow, as a wave in the sea

I continued to spend time in walk moving from one lateral exercise to another until I felt active limbs working well through his back. I tried to keep my rein contact very light during these exercises so that Habil could move through a mobilised back and maintain a natural, relaxed posture within his neck and head. His head and neck came into a good self-carriage from naturally induced engagement.

I then prepared to work in sitting trot with a deeper inhalation and on the outward breath he sprang into an active, elevated trot. This movement felt so different from the initial trot of the warm-up: he had greater cadence and a strong buoyant rhythm with active hind limbs. The change in balance allowed Habil more freedom in his forehand and shoulders. My breathing became tuned to his as I connected with the vibrant elevation in his movement.

We began to experience both connection and collection. As I felt his joy and pride, we connected with the flow of *joie de vivre* and harmony and experienced a true feeling of dance.

We began to experience both connection and collection

We experience a true feeling of dance

We connected with the flow of *joie de vivre* and harmony and experienced a true feeling of dance.

Chapter 7

Epilogue

Lessons from Delfin – the professor

This book has been inspired by, and with grateful thanks to, the many students who have come to me to explore further their journey of horsemanship. I often receive messages saying that something very special was experienced when working with my stallion Delfin. He showed them a connection they had never dreamt was possible between human and horse. I cannot speak highly enough of my stallion, if he were human he would be a highly acclaimed professor willing to share his knowledge for the advancement of humankind.

Overleaf is a small part of a message written by Linda, after working with Delfin.

Delfin — if he were human he would be a highly acclaimed professor

Linda's testimonial

I came to you looking for a new perspective on how I could improve my communication with horses. I wanted to be the best person that I could be for the horse in my life now and those yet to come. Little did I realise that you would provide me with so much more.

I knew I was on an exciting journey of discovery but I did not realise I would find ME! That day with you and especially with Delfin's reaction to me made me explore all my notions of who I am (the good, the bad, and the few downright ugly bits too) and who I wanted to be. At first I felt such a failure with Delfin, but then you turned this around into an amazing positive! Well I came away from you absolutely exhausted and yet lighter in spirit than I had been for a very long time. I felt that I had found ME!

> I wanted to be the best person I could be for the horses in my life

Key points

I have listed below some key points which are based on the personal experiences of students training with my stallions. You may find them helpful.

Key points for loose work

- Breathe out negative emotions – feel the release.

- Gain a strong power of intention but follow with subtle communication and aids.

- Learn how to become positive and assertive – not overbearing and dominant.

- Become aware of the importance of personal space and gain the respect of those around us.

- The first discipline is to tune in to ourselves before we try to connect with the horse.

- Tune in to your feelings – not your expectations.

- Emotions can be felt by people and horses around you.

- People look for acceptance and love, horses look for security leadership and calmness.

- People are inhibited: looking for 'right' or 'wrong', fearing failure and rejection.

- Before we can experience success, we experience failure – this is a natural process of learning.

- Release and become as a child – a child of the universe – and embrace what may be revealed. Cultivate a feeling of enjoyment and play.

Tune in to your feelings not your expectations

Emotions can be felt by people and horses around you

Key points for the rider

- Isolate your core muscles and ride from your seat – not your hands and legs.

- 'Allow' the horse to be in natural self-carriage.

- Let go of tightness and restriction – allow energy to 'flow'.

- Mobility is gained through balance, enhanced by core breathing.

- Mobility allows fluidity, which creates 'oneness'.

- Don't just think of riding forwards – ride the horse with uphill energy into his elevated shoulders – 'ride a mountain'.

Ride the horse with uphill energy into elevated shoulders
....

- Inspire and encourage the horse – use natural methods in training to enhance his spirit.

- Any restriction will create tension.

- Allow the horse to move forward without excessive restriction.

- Think of breathing naturally – an energy exchange.

- Ride the horse from back to front.

- Converse with tact; the hands connect with the mind and mouth of your horse.

- Reinforce your convictions; expect the horse to listen.

- Be prepared to receive and listen.

- In order to experience success, we experience failure; a natural process of learning.

- Keep refreshing your self-awareness, 'top to toe'

- Balance and harmony, on every level, is the key.

- Every few minutes ride on a loose rein, breathe and relax.

- Time and patience – for rider and horse

- Just 'be' with the horse, have fun; aim for harmony and lightness. *Enjoy* each moment.

In order to experience success, we experience failure; a natural process of learning.

Thoughts from students

These words were written after Mary had spent several days training with us.

Mary's testimonial

The journey of life takes us further from our 'child within'. Our first years are ones of exploring, gaining enthusiasm for something new and a love of life and adventure. As years pass we look for the 'downsides', the negatives and things that may go wrong.

God gave us all as individuals, personal gifts which we can pass on to others – for their highest good. We are all worthy of these gifts as we are all part of an orchestra – creating harmony – part of the universe.

We are all here to give and to receive but we build a shield or boundary to keep us feeling more safe and secure.

Only when we push the boundaries can we explore and find our true strengths and weakness. Our weakness can then become our time for learning, our powerhouse and strength. Remember the things that stimulated feelings of pleasure and fun as a child. Return to that place and recapture the feeling of spontaneous delight you experienced as a child. Allow fun into your life – find the ability to laugh at yourself too! We have become very serious!

Learn to love – a result of self-acceptance and happiness – this spirit can then be revealed to others.

> God gave us all personal gifts which we can pass on to others – for their highest good

The study below is from Gemma who came to me with her 17.2hh Friesian mare. Gemma seemed extremely disheartened as her mare fought any contact with the reins. The mare seemed rather 'switched off' yet I sensed that underneath her apathy lay a more sensitive nature.

Gemma's testimonial

Before I met Jenny I had filed away my dreams of dressage and had not been in a manege for two years. I have had my Friesian mare, Welmoed, for five years now. She is my first horse and I had lessons on her with a mainstream instructor for two years but never seemed to be getting to where I wanted to be. My instructor, however, was pleased with our progress as, after all, Welmoed had had no schooling at all before she came to me and I was a novice rider. But I did not feel my horse enjoyed our lessons and this troubled me.

Welmoed was labelled lazy and I was advised to use spurs, a different bit, a bungee to keep her head down, etc. Welmoed seemed to resent contact so much and became so resistant that eventually I stopped schooling altogether and just hacked out on the moors in a head collar, rebuilding my relationship with her.

My first lesson with Jenny was what she calls the 'top to toe'. Whilst practising postures of core stability and all-over relaxation, I was amazed how much tension I carried with me and how obvious it was to Jenny. It was actually really challenging to keep my jaw, neck and shoulders relaxed but as Jenny explained things it became so obvious: if a horse can feel a fly landing, of course they will respond differently when their rider's back is hollowed or rounded!

I was quite anxious about taking Welmoed to Jenny's the first time as she is very sensitive to new environments and, although outwardly she seems calm, she gets tense and rigid, and I was envisaging my old frustrations of a horse who didn't want to move.

Jenny asked if she could loose school Welly to introduce herself and the indoor school and after only a few minutes of tense, high-headed trotting around with reluc-

→

tance, my mare relaxed and, shortly after, was following Jenny around attentively with the soft expression on her face I never thought I'd see during any form of schooling.

Jenny's accurate and speedy assessment of my mare's character as, 'really sensitive and willing as long as she is asked politely; tries hard but gets offended if asked rudely or pushed' made me feel so much better. It wasn't just me that thought that! I had always believed that 'making' her do things or getting 'tougher' with her made things worse, but Jenny was the first instructor I'd had who read her as I do and knew what approach she needed to make progress.

We start each of our sessions with some loose work, which seems to really help Welmoed relax, both physically and mentally, before a ridden session and to start with a better connection between horse and rider. Under Jenny's tuition I have learnt how to lose the tension that builds up in me when Welly isn't going as I would like her to (a situation that rapidly gets worse on all counts for both parties!) and how little changes in my body make a huge difference to the horse.

We have been working on suppling exercises at the walk and very quickly Welmoed is better able to use her hind legs, stepping under herself more evenly and with less effort. Just a few of the exercises at walk seem to have an instant effect on the quality of her trot.

Welly and I have had five lessons with Jenny now and the difference is incredible. Welmoed is softly accepting contact, willingly moving forward, relaxing and stretching very early in a session and seems to enjoy our lessons. It is early days in our learning but I finally feel as if my horse is with me, and now when Jenny talks me through an exercise and adds, 'this is preparation for the pirouette' I can actually envisage Welmoed and I doing such things. Before learning about riding from the core and seeing the changes

Learn to lose the tension that builds up in you

in my horse that I had seen during my training with Jenny, I couldn't picture anything other than my own frustrations where riding with contact was concerned.

I have had the privilege of riding Maestu on the lunge and loose schooling Delfin, as well as seeing Jenny work with her horses. I have felt the energy and seen these beautiful animals moving with joy and exuberance and I am so glad that the dream I had of dancing with a willing and happy horse has become possible.

Gemma with Welmoed, who learns to accept a steady contact, finding harmony and balance in her work

When you read these words you will understand how students and clients have been such an inspiration to me. You cannot progress along the path of horsemanship without understanding this journey, so eloquently described by Mary and Gemma. Riding is not just technical or mechanical but encompasses every level of human awareness.

Riding encompasses every level of human awareness

We cannot be more effective as riders than our personality, experience and state of mind will allow. Our riding can only reflect our true spirit and the relationship we develop with the horse. If the rider becomes disciplined in daily life to move with more balance and grace this will support their riding. Personal posture, supported by core breathing, will be improved by regular practice in everyday tasks. Start to feel the changes, for instance, if you are in a stressful situation, note the changes taking place within your body and breathing. Then, become your own master and sigh deeply, with a natural awareness of more grounded energy.

The discipline is to be aware of changes before we ride, so that a calm and focused mind can become a part of our daily routine.

The key points to remember are:

1. **Top-to-toe** posture awareness

2. Focus on **core breathing** for connection

3. **Visualisation** – to capture the essence of the moment

4. Become the image for the horse to mirror.

Follow in the trail of his hoof prints

Give to the horse patience, love and wisdom together with humility and honesty. You will receive the greatest friendship, trust and courage from the horse. Together, you can build a quiet place for mutual calm where truth from the heart may be nurtured. It is difficult to describe the depth of friendship that the horse can offer, but it has the potential to become both life changing and life enhancing.

The way we ride the horse will be a reflection of the whole relationship that will weave a path to oneness and harmony.

Enjoy the challenge and, with faith and hope, take a step forward to explore all the possibilities. **Secrets of the horse will be given clarity as you go not where the path may lead, but follow in the trail of his hoof prints.**

Give to the horse patience, love and wisdom

Christians Against Poverty

Join Jenny in supporting the much-needed work of the charity, **Christians Against Poverty** (CAP). Jenny supports the charity with donations from the income from her teaching, books and DVDs, and with publicity.

Christians Against Poverty is a national debt-counselling charity with a network of over 150 centres based in local churches. CAP offers hope and a solution to anyone in debt through its unique, in-depth service.

CAP provides sustainable poverty relief through a combination of award-winning debt counselling, specialist advice and practical help. CAP's unique 'hands on' approach empowers people to help themselves out of poverty and be released from the fear, oppression and worry generated by overwhelming debts. CAP's service teaches clients vital budgeting skills that will last a lifetime, and help future generations avoid debt.

The charity began in 1996 when John Kirkby, armed with a £10 donation and a passion for those in need, started to help people in his local community who were trapped in debt. Now, it is a fast-paced, growing organisation whose vision is to answer the national problem of debt in the UK by having at least one CAP Debt Centre operating in every major town and city by the year 2015. Since 1996, over 45,000 people have been helped by the organisation.

For more information about Christians Against Poverty, visit www.capuk.org.

Index